The SPSS® Book

The SPSS® Book

A Student Guide to the Statistical Package
for the Social Sciences®

Matthew J. Zagumny, Ph.D.

Writers Club Press
San Jose New York Lincoln Shanghai

Writers Club Press
an imprint of iUniverse.com, Inc.

For information address:
iUniverse.com, Inc.
5220 S 16th, Ste. 200
Lincoln, NE 68512
www.iuniverse.com

Cover photo by Matthew J. Zagumny

ISBN: 0-595-18913-X

Printed in the United States of America

To my loving Luddite, Lisa. Thank you!

CONTENTS

INTRODUCTION

I wrote this manual to present a simple guide to the use of the Statistical Package for the Social Sciences®, the most common statistical analysis program available. The procedures described and the interpretation of the results of various statistical analyses comes from my 14 years of experience as a student and teacher of statistics and SPSS®. This manual, written in plain and straightforward language, can be used as a supplement to a textbook for undergraduate and graduate statistics courses or as a stand-alone manual. I wrote *The SPSS® Book* with the undergraduate student of statistics in mind. Each chapter should be used comprehensively in order to gain the full benefit of understanding the SPSS® procedures and the reasoning behind their use and results. The book also includes step-by-step instructions on the use of the SPSS® pull-down menus for each of the statistical procedures covered. As an added benefit, I have included a comprehensive index to assure that *The SPSS® Book* can be efficiently and effectively used as a reference manual. This manual will demystify statistical computing and reinforce important elements of statistical reasoning typically covered in undergraduate and graduate statistics and research methods courses.

To help you use this book more effectively, I have used particular notations to represent either SPSS® features or variable names that we must specify in data and syntax files. SPSS® features are always reported in quotation marks (e.g., "Define Variables" window) and variable names are reported in all capital letters (e.g., GENDER). It is best to read the entire chapter, but the reader can also read just a section of each chapter.

My hope is that this book will make statistics and SPSS® easier for students to use and understand.

Happy computing!

Chapter 1: Windows® and SPSS® Basics

Window® Basics

Before we actually get to entering data and running a command there are a couple of important points about Windows® that you need to know. The windows button at the top of your screen (the screen is call the 'desktop' in Windows® lingo) that has an "X" in it, will close the active file (i.e., the file that is 'highlighted'). So if you want to remove one of your files from the desktop (screen), place your mouse cursor (i.e., the arrow) on the "X" button and click the left mouse button. This will close out that file and remove it from your desktop. The button immediately to the left of 'close window' button is the 'restore window' button (the button that has a square or window icon). No this doesn't restore the files you close. It will either reduce or enlarge the area that the active file takes on your screen.

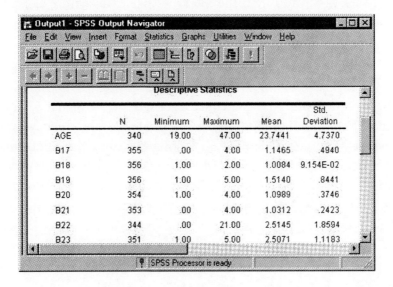

Figure 1.1: A SPSS® Output Window

Depending on how your system is set up, SPSS® may open the data file so it is already enlarged. If this is the case, this 'restore windows' button will have two squares or window icons in it. If SPSS® opens the data file up in a cascade format (when you can see both the data and syntax files), then there will be only one large windows icon in the button. When you are using a particular file, it is best to have that file enlarged so that it takes up the entire area of your screen. That way you can see more of what you're working on. When your done working with a particular file (like when your done entering data or finished writing your command in the syntax file) reduce the file back down to the cascade format so you can work with the other files. The third and final button up in the right hand corner of your windows is a dash or underline or hyphen or some sort of straight line (call it whatever you want), which has the official name 'minimize window.' If you click on this button, the active file will be 'minimized' or placed down on the 'task bar' at the bottom of your Windows desktop. The button will have the file name followed by 'SPSS' and then the file type (like data, syntax or output). You can 'maximize' the window again by clicking on the button with 'SPSS ... 'on it (See Figure 1.1).

SPSS® Basics

The structure of SPSS (Statistical Package for the Social Sciences)® includes three files (See Figure 1.2): (1) A data file which always has the extension (*.sav). You'll notice that along the top of the data matrix there are gray boxes with the word 'var' in the box. These are where the variable names will be named. Variables always are listed across the top of the data file (i.e., columns) and cases are listed down the side of the data file (i.e., rows). (2) A syntax file which always has the extension(*.sps). This is our command file or if you want to talk like an engineer or computer geek you can say "this is where we are writing code." Each SPSS® command has a certain syntax or structure-the commands are very easy to write and in most cases we will just use the pull-down menus. (3) An output file which has the extension (*.spo). This file will show us the results of the statistical analysis that we run. This file will be created by SPSS® so you don't need to worry about creating this file.

So the flow of work using SPSS® is that you enter the data you collected into the data file, then you write a command in the syntax file (or use the pull-down menus to generate the commands), run the command, and then go look at the results in the output file (which is generated for you once SPSS® has calculated the results).

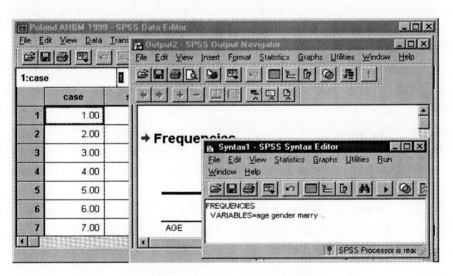

Figure 1.2: SPSS® 3 File Structure

Creating a data file

Now we are ready to enter our first data file. First place your disk in the floppy drive (make sure it's formatted). Now let's think of a study that we can collect data for…usually this process is long and sometimes painful. As you begin to conduct your own research, you will find that at times developing research questions can be difficult. But for this example let's study if a person's age is related to whether he or she believes that Elvis is alive.

Naming variables

To create the data file we need to first identify which variables we will be measuring. To name a variable in SPSS®, the name must be 8 characters or less and be one word (no spaces, dashes, etc.). We can use numbers in our variable names but we cannot start a variable name with a number. It's important to remember that variable names must be all one word! The first variable in our data file should be a participant number or "SUBNUM." Why is it important to number our participants? So we can keep track of who is giving us which data. I have a perfect example of why it's so important. We were doing some research in Poland with college students. Over the summer a student was working with me to enter the data. When we ran the statistics, we found out that something came out weird. So like good researchers, we went back to the data file and found that data was entered as '15' for a scale that had a possible range of '1' to '6.' A common mistake in data entry; the fingers are sometimes too fast for their own good! Out of over 500 surveys it would have been almost impossible to figure out which survey the error came from if we had not numbered our subjects' surveys. We went to the hard copy of the survey and quickly found out what the entry should have been. So the take home lesson: NUMBER YOUR PARTIC-IPANTS AND THEIR DATA!

In all types of research, it is important to collect sociodemographic information about your participants, such as gender, race, age, etc. For the current research about whether people think Elvis is alive, we will need to collect data on the age of our participants. To make a strong argument for this association, we will also need to collect other data to determine if there may be some other reason for the relationship-like maybe older people get better drugs, or maybe it just so happens that fewer younger people live near Memphis and so don't believe in the 'walking Elvis.' All of these are possible explanations for the relationship between age and belief in the 'living Elvis.' So after the SUBNUM the next variable will be BELIEVE. This variable will be coded so that '1' will be used for those who do not believe Elvis is alive and '2' for those who believe he is alive. What level of measurement is this? It's nominal or categorical. The variable only tells us which group or category participants belong to, either 'non- believers' (1) or 'believers' (2). Now let's collect data on AGE. We would probably collect the age of our participants anyway, but for our current research we would want to collect this data to see if AGE is related to belief in the living Elvis. AGE is what level of measurement? That's right, ratio level of measurement! Just to keep it simple to start, these are the only variables for which we will collect data.

Defining Variables

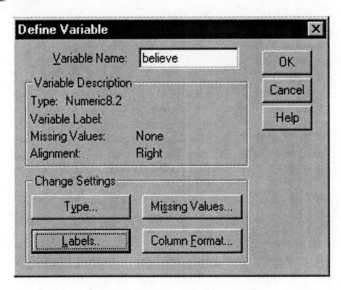

Figure 1.3: Define Variable Window

Let's now define the variable names we have chosen. Using the mouse, place the arrow cursor on the first gray box that has "VAR." Double click the left mouse button and the "Define Variable" window will open (See Figure 1.3). The variable name is highlighted so we can just type the name of the first variable name, which should always be SUBNUM. We must also identify the appropriate level of measurement for the variables in the data file. SUBNUM is nominal because the value of the variable only designates that one case is different than all of the others (this is sometimes called categorical). Once you have this variable name typed in and the nominal level of measurement selected, click on the OK button. This closes the "Define Variable" window. Notice the first gray box in the data file now has SUBNUM instead of VAR. We're going to do the same thing for the next variable. Double click on the gray box at the top of the second column and the "Define Variable" window comes up. Type in the name of the second variable, BELIEVE. There is more to this variable than just a subject number.

Menu Commands

> >Double click "VAR" box
> >Type in variable name
> >   >Select the level of measurement
> >OK

Variable Labels and Value Labels

So, let's click on the "Labels" button. There are two type of labels we can use in SPSS®. A "Variable Label" allows us to describe the variable within 60 spaces. If I didn't know what research you were working on, I would see the BELIEVE variable name and not have any idea what you were studying. The Variable Label aids in the description of the variable names. Type "Is Elvis alive?" in the Variable Label box.

The second type of label is a Value Label. This allows us to define the values that a variable can have. For BELIEVE the possible values are '1' and '2.' So, in the Value box type '1' and then hit the 'Tab' key so that the cursor is in the 'Label' box and then type "No." (If you remember, we decided that people who do not believe that Elvis is alive would be coded 1 and believers would be coded 2.) Click on the 'Add' button, so that the value label for '1' appears in the box at the bottom of the Labels window (See Figure 1.4). Using your mouse click on the Value box and enter '2.' Again, using the 'Tab' key move the cursor to the Label box (you can also use the mouse to click the cursor in the Label box). Type in "Yes." Again, click on the 'Add' button. Don't forget to click on the 'Add' button after every value you label. If for some reason you forget, SPSS® will prompt you when you click on the OK button. Once you have both values labeled and they appear in the box that the bottom of the window, click on the 'Continue' button. This brings us back to the 'Define Variable' window. Notice the variable label is listed in the middle of this window. Click on the "OK" button.

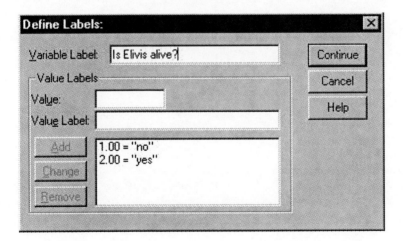

Figure 1.4: Define Labels Window

Let's define the next variable by double clicking the third gray box. This variable is AGE, so type AGE in the variable name. Click on the 'Labels' button again, but this time we will only add a variable label (let's use "Age of participant"). Since age is a continuously measured variable we will not use value labels; the values of this variable are self-explanatory. Now our data file is all set up to start entering data.

Entering Data

To enter data in the data file, first of course, make sure the data file is 'active,' which you will be able to tell by seeing the highlighted bar along the top. Next, make sure that the data box at the top left of the data file is highlighted with black around it. We will enter the number '1' first because this is the first subject. Notice your entry appears at the top of the data file. This gives you a chance to change the entry if you have accidentally entered the wrong data. Simply use the right arrow key on your keyboard to move to the next data box, which is the BELIEVE variable. Once you move the highlighted box to the next data box, the '1' you entered will appear in the first data box. You can also move the highlighted box using your mouse. Let's enter all the data listed below so it looks like the data file in Figure1.5.

SUBNUM	BELIEVE	AGE
1	1	21
2	1	28
3	1	31
4	1	29
5	1	28
6	2	43
7	2	38
8	2	59
9	2	78
10	2	59

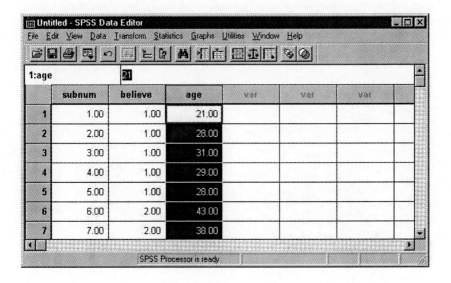

Figure 1.5: SPSS® Data File

So now we have our first data file! Yeah!

Saving Files

Next we'll learn to save a file. Place your floppy disk in the disk drive. Open up the 'File' menu and click on 'Save As.' The 'Save Data As' window comes up (Figure 1.6). We need to come up with a file name. For our example let's use 'Elvis and age' as our file name. Notice at the bottom of this window that the file type is an SPSS® data file because it has the *.SAV

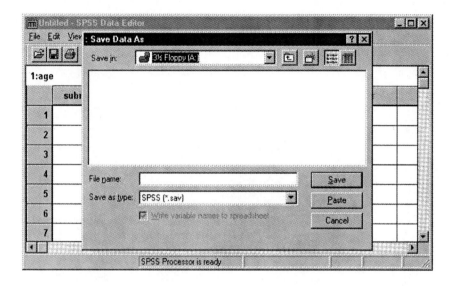

Figure 1.6: Saving a File

extension. Make sure that the drive where you are saving your file is the proper disk drive (usually A:/ drive). SPSS® automatically saves the file extension with the file name you typed in. So you will be able to quickly identify the data file from your disk directory.

Frequencies Command and Output

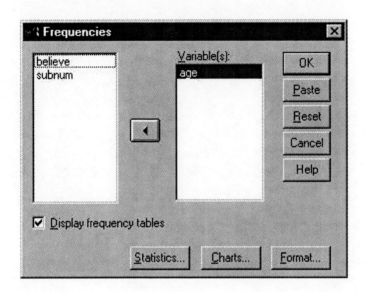

Figure 1.7: Frequencies Window

Now let's run some statistics on our data file! Yea! Click on the 'Statistics' option in the word menu to pull down the statistics menu. Let's do some frequencies and descriptives. Click on the 'Summarize' button and the descriptives menu opens up. First click on 'Frequencies.' The 'Frequencies' window displays the names of all of our defined variables in our data file, on the left hand side of the window (See Figure 1.7). The box on the right hand side of this window, titled "Variables,' will list only those variables for which SPSS® will develop a frequency distribution. You can double click on the variable name or just single click to highlight the variable name and then click on the black arrow button. To remove a variable from the 'Variable' list, highlight it and click on the black arrow button to place it back on the left

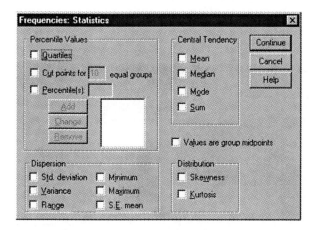

Figure 1.8: Statistics Subcommand Window

hand side of the window. For this exercise, let's get a frequency distribution for all of the variables in our data file.

Statistics Subcommand

Once you have all of the variable names listed in the 'Variable' list, click on the 'Statistics' button. There are descriptive statistics available for percentiles, central tendency measures, and dispersion (See Figure 1.8). At a minimum you will always want the mean and standard deviation. Once you have selected all of the statistics you want, click on the 'continue' button and then click on the 'OK' button.

Viewer File (Results)

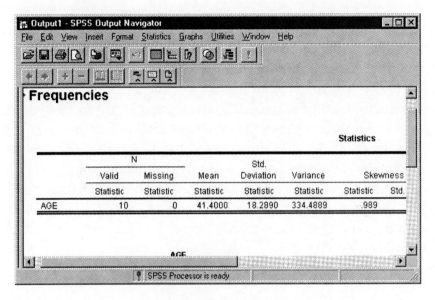

Figure 1.9: Output (Viewer) File

Let's look at the viewer file so, enlarge the window so that the viewer file is as large as your computer screen (See Figure 1.9). You may also want to click and hold on the gray bar the splits the screen vertically and move the bar to the right. Our actual results from running the command are listed on the right-hand side of that gray bar and a directory tree is listed on the left-hand. The directory tree is of no use so to move the gray bar over to the far right will allow you to see more of the actual viewer file.

In the output file, the variable names (or variable label if we used one, like for BELIEVE) appear along the left hand side of the screen. The next column is the valid number of observations, which is 10 for each of our variables. The next column lists the mean of each variable.

For SUBNUM and BELIEVE, a mean does not have any meaning. A mean is only useful for interval or ratio data, not for categorical or nominal data. The next column shows the standard deviation for each of our variables. Again, the standard deviation is useful as a measure of dispersion only for data which is interval or ratio level. Since SUBNUM and BELIEVE are nominal measures, the mean and standard deviation is only useful for the variable AGE (See Figure 1.9). If you scroll down, you will see the frequency distributions for each of the variables. Frequencies are most often run to check that data was entered correctly. For example, in the data from Poland that I was talking about earlier we used a frequencies command to determine if any of the data had been entered incorrectly. Once we saw a value of 15 in the frequency distribution for a survey item that should have had a range of 1-6, we caught our data entry error.

Descriptives Command

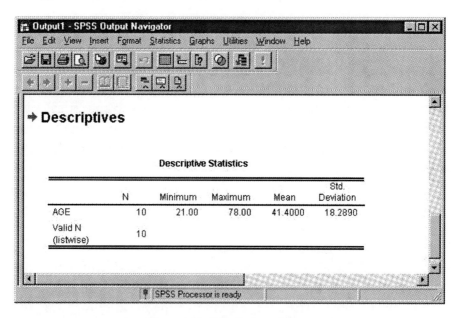

Figure 1.10: Descriptives Output

Now let's run the 'Descriptives' command. Reduce the size of the output window so that you can see all three SPSS® files. Click on the syntax window so that it is active. Click on the 'Statistics' pull-down menu and click on 'Summarize.' This time, instead of clicking on 'Frequencies,' click on 'Descriptives.' The 'Descriptives' window will open up. We would use this command if we wanted just descriptive statistics on a variable. For our example we will only want descriptives on AGE. (Remember that SUBNUM and BELIEVE are nominal data) Double click on AGE so that it moves to the box under 'Variables.' Just like the 'Frequencies' command, this tells SPSS® which variables you want included in the analysis. Next, click on the 'Options' button, which will open the 'Options' window. Click on those descriptive statistics that you want to request. At a minimum you should request the mean (41.40) and standard deviation (18.29). Click on the 'Continue' button and finally click on the 'OK' button. This is to show you the other way to run commands. The results of the analysis are listed at the end of the frequencies in the output file. Scroll to the place where 'Descriptives' are listed. As with the frequencies, the variable name is listed along the left side of the results table followed by the mean and the standard deviation (See Figure 1.10). Notice that the format of the SPSS® command is always the first thing listed in the output window. Don't forget to save the output file with the file name 'Elvis and age.' Remember that you will be able to tell the difference between the data, syntax, and output files by their extension.

Printing a File

In order to print a file you can click on the printer icon in the tool bar or click on "File" in the word menu and then click on "Print." If you want the entire file printed all you need to do is click on the 'OK' button. If you want to print only a part of the file, highlight the part of the file you want to print then go to the 'Print' window, through the 'File' menu, and click on the 'OK' button. If you want to print the whole file or just a part, SPSS® will prompt you after to click the 'OK' button in the 'Print' window. The prompt window will ask you if you want to print the entire file or just the selection. If you have highlighted a part of the file you want to print, the 'Selection' choice will already be selected. If you have not highlighted any parts of the file, the 'Full' choice will already be selected. Now just click on the 'OK' button and get your printout.

Chapter 2: Independent Samples and Matched Samples t-Tests

Independent Samples t-Test: The Research Question

You are researchers interested in examining the effect of type of music on math performance. Specifically, you are interested in whether classical music improves college students' performance on a math test. You decide to use a two group design with people randomly assigned to either an experimental condition that has students listening to U2 (rock treatment condition) or to Mozart (classical treatment group). You randomly assign 30 students to each treatment condition for a total N=60. The participants in each group will listen to their assigned music while completing a test on basic mathematics. We'll measure the math test on a percentage scale with the dependent measure representing the percentage of correct responses (0%-100%).

Independent Samples t-Test: The Data

Enter the following data set generated for this research question into the SPSS® data editor. The independent variable of music is coded with "1" as U2 listeners and "2" as Mozart listeners.

SUBNUM	MUSIC	GRADE
1.00	1.00	47.00
2.00	1.00	43.00
3.00	1.00	39.00
4.00	1.00	53.00
5.00	1.00	42.00
6.00	1.00	56.00

7.00	1.00	53.00
8.00	1.00	52.00
9.00	1.00	46.00
10.00	1.00	45.00
11.00	1.00	44.00
12.00	1.00	53.00
13.00	1.00	39.00
14.00	1.00	53.00
15.00	1.00	62.00
16.00	1.00	45.00
17.00	1.00	56.00
18.00	1.00	41.00
19.00	1.00	46.00
20.00	1.00	48.00
21.00	1.00	57.00
22.00	1.00	54.00
23.00	1.00	45.00
24.00	1.00	51.00
25.00	1.00	62.00
26.00	1.00	44.00
27.00	1.00	55.00
28.00	1.00	38.00
29.00	1.00	56.00
30.00	1.00	36.00
31.00	2.00	72.00
32.00	2.00	77.00
33.00	2.00	90.00
34.00	2.00	88.00
35.00	2.00	80.00
36.00	2.00	82.00
37.00	2.00	85.00
38.00	2.00	74.00

39.00	2.00	93.00
40.00	2.00	86.00
41.00	2.00	93.00
42.00	2.00	86.00
43.00	2.00	96.00
44.00	2.00	77.00
45.00	2.00	88.00
46.00	2.00	72.00
47.00	2.00	90.00
48.00	2.00	90.00
49.00	2.00	94.00
50.00	2.00	71.00
51.00	2.00	97.00
52.00	2.00	97.00
53.00	2.00	82.00
54.00	2.00	87.00
55.00	2.00	85.00
56.00	2.00	83.00
57.00	2.00	81.00
58.00	2.00	78.00
59.00	2.00	92.00
60.00	2.00	93.00

Independent Samples t-Test: The Command

Syntax Command

We can run the independent samples t—test command using either written command language or through the pull-down menus. The written syntax for the independent samples t—test is as follows:

```
T-TEST
GROUPS=music(1 2)
/MISSING=ANALYSIS
```

/VARIABLES=grade
/CRITERIA=CIN(.99) .

Where MUSIC is the name of the independent variable and GRADE is the name of the dependent variable.

Menu Command:

To conduct the independent samples t—test on the data in this chapter (of course, after entering the data), click on the "Statistics" pull-down menu, and then "Compare Means," and then "Independent-Samples T-Test." (See Figure 2.1)

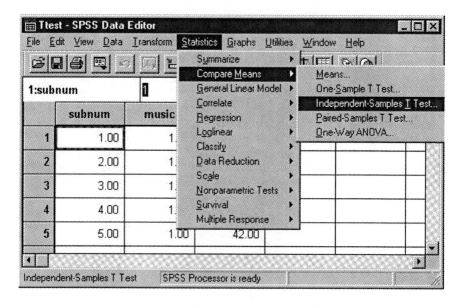

Figure 2.1: Pull-Down Menu for Independent-Samples t-Test

The Independent-Samples T-Test window will open. We need to select the "Test Variable(s)" or the dependent variable in our study. Select the dependent variable by clicking on the variable name

"GRADE" and then click on the black arrow button next to the "Test Variable(s)" windowpane. Next, we must select the "Grouping Variable" or independent variable. For our study the independent variable is "MUSIC," so highlight the "MUSIC" variable name and click on the black arrow button next to the "Grouping Variable" windowpane. Next we must define the levels of the independent variable by clicking on the "Define Groups" button. In the "Define Groups" window, type 1 in the "Group 1" box and 2 in the "Group 2" box (See Figure 2.2). We coded the U2 listeners as "1" and Mozart listeners as "2," so we need to identify the coding of the two research groups for SPSS®. Once you have identified the research group coding in the "Define Groups" window, click on the "Continue" button. Now we are ready to run the independent-samples t—test by clicking the "OK" button in the "Independent-Samples T-Test window (and the output window pops up with results!). It's a lot easier than conducting t—tests by hand, isn't it!?!

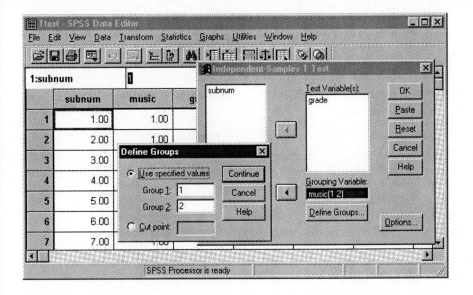

Figure 2.2: Defining the Independent-Samples t–Test Variables and Groups.

>Statistics
>Compare Means
>Independent-Samples T Test
>[Select dependent variable for "Test Variable(s)"]
>[Select independent variable for "Grouping Variable"]
>Define Groups
>[Type in codes for both treatment groups in the panes provided]
>Continue
>OK

Independent Samples t-Test: Interpreting the Results

The independent samples t -Test output includes 2 tables. The first table lists the "Group Statistics," including the sample size (N), treatment mean, standard deviation (Std. Deviation), and standard error of the mean for each treatment condition (See Figure 2.3). The treatment means will allow us to determine which of the two groups performed significantly better on the math test, *if the independent samples t—test shows that there was a significant difference between the two groups.*

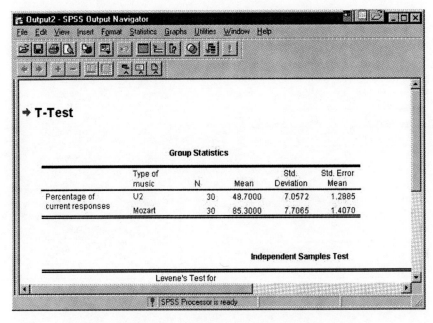

Figure 2.3: Output File for Independent-Samples t -Test

The second table is called the "Independent Samples Test" and includes two separate sections (See Figure 2.4). The first section, printed on the left-hand side of the table, lists the results of "Levene's Test for the Equality of Variances" or otherwise known as a test for the homogeneity of variance assumption. This assumption states that the variances of the two treatment populations are equal: $s_1{}^2 = s_2{}^2$. To evaluate Levene's test we compare the value listed under "Sig." to our alpha level (.05 or .01, whichever you are using). In our example, the significance level reported under Levene's test is .788 which is greater than our a=.01, therefore, we did not brake the assumption of homogeneity of variances. If the "Sig." value listed under Levene's test was less than our decision rule (a=.01), we would have broken the assumption of homogeneity. Next we'll examine the right-hand side of the second table in the output; the "t—test for Equality of Means."

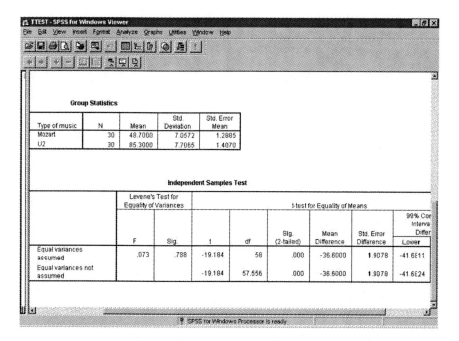

Figure 2.4: Results of Independent-Samples t-Test

Since we did not brake the assumption of homogeneity in our example, we will interpret the top row of the "Equality of Means" table. This top row is headed "Equal variances assumed." This portion of the table lists the t value, degrees of freedom (df = n_1 + n_2 -2), the significance level of t—test (Sig. 2-tailed), mean difference (M_1—M_2), the standard error of the difference (Std. Error Difference: S_{x1-x2}), and the confidence intervals for the differences between the treatment means with "Lower" and "Upper" confidence intervals.

To evaluate the significance of the t—test we compare the significance level reported under "Sig. (2-tailed)" with our decision rule (a=.01). For our music example, the calculated significance level was .000, which is interpreted as .001. Since the calculated significance level is less than the decision rule of .01, we would reject the null (H_0) and conclude that there is a significant difference between the two treatment populations. Remember that the null hypothesis states the two treatment population means are equal (i.e. $m_1 = m_2$). Since we rejected the null hypothesis, we are concluding that $m_1 \neq m_2$. We now examine the treatment means and see that those students who listened to Mozart performed significantly better on the math test than those students who listened to U2.

Since we found a significant *t*—test result we would report the findings as follow:

Those students who listened to Mozart music ($M = 85.3, SD = 7.71$) while studying performed significantly better on the math test than those students who listened to U2 music ($M = 48.7, SD = 7.06$) while studying, $t(58) = -19.18, p < .001$.

Notice that the means (*M*) and standard deviations (*SD*) from the "Group Statistics" table are reported immediately following the mention of the treatment groups in the research conclusion. Also notice that the correct method for reporting the *t*—test results is to include the degrees of freedom (df=58), *t* value (*t*=19.18), and the calculated significance level ($p < .001$).

Independent Samples t -Test: Further Practice

We are researching the effects of green M&Ms ® on sexual arousal. We randomly assign people to one of two treatment conditions: (1) people who will eat green M&Ms ®; or (2) people who will eat red M&Ms ®. After we give the designated M&Ms ® to the study participants, we will measure their sexual arousal. We could measure sexual arousal in a number of different ways (just use your imagination!), but for this study we will measure it using a 0-10 (0= no sexual arousal and 10=very high sexual arousal). Remember that SPSS® only allows variable names of 8 characters or less, so use the following variable names.

SUBNUM	MandM	SA (Sexual Arousal)
1.00	1.00	7.00
2.00	1.00	7.00
3.00	1.00	10.00
4.00	1.00	8.00
5.00	1.00	9.00
6.00	1.00	8.00
7.00	1.00	9.00
8.00	1.00	8.00
9.00	1.00	9.00
10.00	1.00	7.00
11.00	1.00	7.00
12.00	1.00	8.00
13.00	1.00	8.00
14.00	1.00	7.00
15.00	1.00	9.00
16.00	1.00	9.00
17.00	1.00	7.00
18.00	1.00	7.00
19.00	1.00	7.00
20.00	1.00	9.00
21.00	1.00	6.00
22.00	1.00	9.00
23.00	1.00	9.00
24.00	1.00	9.00
25.00	1.00	6.00
26.00	1.00	9.00
27.00	1.00	9.00
28.00	1.00	8.00

29.00	1.00	7.00
30.00	1.00	10.00
31.00	2.00	5.00
32.00	2.00	3.00
33.00	2.00	6.00
34.00	2.00	2.00
35.00	2.00	4.00
36.00	2.00	4.00
37.00	2.00	4.00
38.00	2.00	5.00
39.00	2.00	4.00
40.00	2.00	6.00
41.00	2.00	4.00
42.00	2.00	6.00
43.00	2.00	5.00
44.00	2.00	3.00
45.00	2.00	2.00
46.00	2.00	5.00
47.00	2.00	4.00
48.00	2.00	3.00
49.00	2.00	4.00
50.00	2.00	4.00
51.00	2.00	4.00
52.00	2.00	6.00
53.00	2.00	6.00
54.00	2.00	4.00
55.00	2.00	4.00
56.00	2.00	5.00
57.00	2.00	3.00
58.00	2.00	3.00
59.00	2.00	5.00
60.00	2.00	5.00

After running the SPSS® independent samples t—test analysis, write up the results for an APA style results section.

Paired Samples t-Test: The Research Question

For the matched samples t-test, lets examine the effects of alcohol on driving ability. We will utilize a pretest-posttest design, where we will measure driving ability, have participants drink the equivalent of 4 oz of liquor, and then drive again on a closed-circuit driving course. We will measure driving ability as the number of orange course cones that are hit by the participant (0-20). Of course, we would have to assure that our participants were completely sober before we dismissed them from the study.

Paired Samples t-Test: The Data

Following is the data for our drinking and driving study. Notice that we have selected 30 total subjects. This is because the Central Limit Theorem states that a sample size of 30 or greater is generally needed in order to assume a normally distributed sampling distribution.

SUBNUM	PRETEST	POSTTEST
1.00	11.00	18.00
2.00	11.00	17.00
3.00	13.00	14.00
4.00	10.00	17.00
5.00	14.00	16.00
6.00	7.00	13.00
7.00	9.00	18.00
8.00	12.00	19.00
9.00	11.00	14.00
10.00	9.00	14.00
11.00	9.00	15.00
12.00	5.00	14.00

13.00	9.00	17.00
14.00	10.00	17.00
15.00	7.00	15.00
16.00	11.00	17.00
17.00	10.00	19.00
18.00	11.00	20.00
19.00	7.00	17.00
20.00	9.00	13.00
21.00	11.00	14.00
22.00	5.00	18.00
23.00	9.00	16.00
24.00	9.00	20.00
25.00	11.00	15.00
26.00	6.00	15.00
27.00	12.00	15.00
28.00	9.00	15.00
29.00	9.00	15.00
30.00	10.00	16.00

Paired Samples t-Test: The Command

Syntax Command

Following is the syntax command. This was created using the pull-down menu command described below.

```
T-TEST
PAIRS= pretest WITH posttest (PAIRED)
/CRITERIA=CIN(.95)
/MISSING=ANALYSIS.
```

Where PRETEST and POSTTEST are the two levels of the paired samples variable.

Menu Command

To provide examples of both older versions (v8.0) and the latest version of SPSS® (v10.0), the following menu command description involves using figures from version 10.0. The independent samples example in the first part of this chapter was described using version 8.0.

To request the paired samples t-test procedure, click on "Analyze" in the word menu, then "Compare Means," followed by "Paired Samples *T*-Test" (See Figure 2.5). This opens the "Paired Samples *T*-Test" window. Next select the levels of the paired samples by clicking on each variables name listed in the windowpane on the left of the "Paired Samples" window. Notice that the variable names appear next to the "Variable 1:" and "Variable 2:" listing in the bottom left-hand corner of the window (i.e. in the "Current Selections" box). Once you have identified the appropriate levels of the variable, click on the black arrow button. The level names will appear in the right-hand windowpane (i.e., "PRETEST-POSTTEST"). Once you have identified the levels, click on the "OK" button and SPSS® will run the *t*-test.

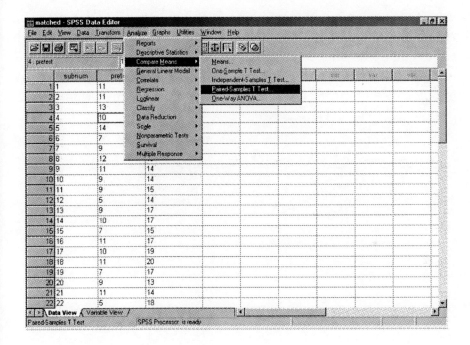

Figure 2.5: Selecting the Paired Samples *T*-Test Procedure

Paired Samples t-Test: Interpreting the Results

The result of the paired samples t-test procedure includes three tables (See Figure 2.6). The first table reports the means, sample sizes, standard deviations, and standard error of the mean. We also report the means and standard deviations of all our treatment groups in our research manuscripts, so this table is very useful. In fact, you'll see that in every chapter of this book that we request means and standard deviations for each of the treatment conditions, regardless of the results of the statistical testing. The next table reports the correlation between the PRETEST and POSTTEST scores. The last table reports the results of the paired samples t-test. To interpret the results we compare the "Sig."

value reported at the far right of the SPSS® Viewer file to our decision rule (a = .01). Since the significance level reported in ".000," we interpret the calculated significance level to be .001. The calculated significance level of .001 is less than our decision rule of .01, therefore the paired samples t-test is statistically significant. This means that we would reject the null hypothesis (H_0: $m_D = 0$).

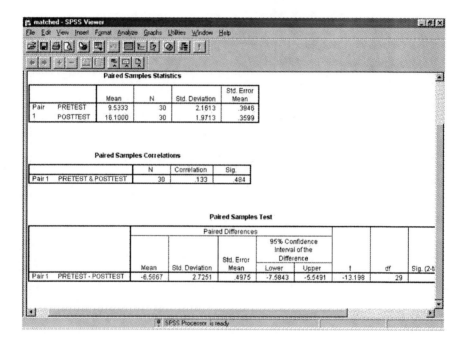

Figure 2.6: Results of the Paired Samples t-Test Procedure

Since we found a significant *t* statistic, we report the results in the following APA format.

Results of the pretest-posttest designed demonstrated that partici-pants hit a significantly greater number of traffic cones after consuming

4oz of alcohol (M=16.1, SD=1.97) than before consuming the alcohol (M=9.53, SD=2.16), t (29) = -13.2, p < .001.

Notice that the means and standard deviations for each measurement period are reported immediately following the mention of the level. Also note that the results of the t-test are reported with the degrees of freedom, the value of the t statistic, and the significance level reported by SPSS®.

Paired Samples t-Test: Further Practice

Let's examine the effects of marijuana on driving ability. We will use the same dependent variable measure of the number of traffic cones the participants hit and the same pretest-posttest design. Analyze the following data using the paired samples t-test procedure. What do you conclude about the effect of marijuana on driving ability? Write up the results of the study in APA format.

SUBNUM	PRETEST	POSTTEST
1.00	8.00	16.00
2.00	13.00	19.00
3.00	9.00	18.00
4.00	9.00	16.00
5.00	13.00	19.00
6.00	8.00	18.00
7.00	8.00	12.00
8.00	10.00	14.00
9.00	9.00	14.00
10.00	10.00	15.00
11.00	10.00	19.00
12.00	10.00	18.00
13.00	10.00	18.00
14.00	13.00	17.00

15.00	7.00	16.00
16.00	12.00	17.00
17.00	6.00	15.00
18.00	7.00	20.00
19.00	10.00	15.00
20.00	9.00	15.00
21.00	12.00	18.00
22.00	7.00	19.00
23.00	10.00	16.00
24.00	11.00	17.00
25.00	8.00	14.00
26.00	8.00	16.00
27.00	6.00	16.00
28.00	8.00	19.00
29.00	10.00	15.00
30.00	6.00	14.00

Chapter 3: One-way Analysis of Variance

One-Way ANOVA: The Research Question

As researchers you are interesting in the effects of LIVING SITUATION on course GRADES in a college statistics course. Now, we could not ethically randomly assign people to a particular living situation, but let's pretend we can! How many students will we need for each LIVING SITUATION? 30!!! Why 30? Because the Central Limit Theorem states that the sample size for each treatment condition must have at least 30 participants in order for the resulting sampling distribution to be normally distributed.

How many LIVING SITUATIONS should we use for this experiment? Let's use four (4), which will include the following *levels* of the independent variable called LIVING SITUATION: (1) *Dorm*; (2) *Apartment with roommates*; (3) *Apartment without roommates*; and (4) *Living with Parents*. We will measure the dependent variable, STATISTICS GRADE, as a percentage of the total test points for that semester, so the dependent variable will range in scores from 0% to 100%.

One-Way ANOVA: The Data

Enter the following data set generated for this research question into the SPSS® data editor.

SUBNUM	LIVING	GRADE
1.00	1.00	60.00
2.00	1.00	54.00
3.00	1.00	54.00
4.00	1.00	56.00

5.00	1.00	40.00
6.00	1.00	51.00
7.00	1.00	35.00
8.00	1.00	59.00
9.00	1.00	57.00
10.00	1.00	55.00
11.00	1.00	43.00
12.00	1.00	47.00
13.00	1.00	57.00
14.00	1.00	48.00
15.00	1.00	49.00
16.00	1.00	45.00
17.00	1.00	55.00
18.00	1.00	54.00
19.00	1.00	50.00
20.00	1.00	35.00
21.00	1.00	46.00
22.00	1.00	54.00
23.00	1.00	57.00
24.00	1.00	63.00
25.00	1.00	52.00
26.00	1.00	45.00
27.00	1.00	49.00
28.00	1.00	61.00
29.00	1.00	38.00
30.00	1.00	42.00
31.00	2.00	61.00
32.00	2.00	55.00
33.00	2.00	58.00
34.00	2.00	50.00
35.00	2.00	55.00
36.00	2.00	37.00

37.00	2.00	64.00
38.00	2.00	60.00
39.00	2.00	46.00
40.00	2.00	53.00
41.00	2.00	42.00
42.00	2.00	45.00
43.00	2.00	55.00
44.00	2.00	40.00
45.00	2.00	53.00
46.00	2.00	40.00
47.00	2.00	46.00
48.00	2.00	51.00
49.00	2.00	48.00
50.00	2.00	51.00
51.00	2.00	43.00
52.00	2.00	55.00
53.00	2.00	35.00
54.00	2.00	43.00
55.00	2.00	47.00
56.00	2.00	41.00
57.00	2.00	41.00
58.00	2.00	64.00
59.00	2.00	49.00
60.00	2.00	50.00
61.00	3.00	60.00
62.00	3.00	45.00
63.00	3.00	49.00
64.00	3.00	56.00
65.00	3.00	49.00
66.00	3.00	51.00
67.00	3.00	62.00
68.00	3.00	47.00

69.00	3.00	39.00
70.00	3.00	51.00
71.00	3.00	56.00
72.00	3.00	35.00
73.00	3.00	59.00
74.00	3.00	45.00
75.00	3.00	43.00
76.00	3.00	49.00
77.00	3.00	56.00
78.00	3.00	54.00
79.00	3.00	49.00
80.00	3.00	48.00
81.00	3.00	59.00
82.00	3.00	44.00
83.00	3.00	52.00
84.00	3.00	45.00
85.00	3.00	53.00
86.00	3.00	42.00
87.00	3.00	46.00
88.00	3.00	51.00
89.00	3.00	56.00
90.00	3.00	51.00
91.00	4.00	84.00
92.00	4.00	85.00
93.00	4.00	83.00
94.00	4.00	77.00
95.00	4.00	88.00
96.00	4.00	90.00
97.00	4.00	88.00
98.00	4.00	94.00
99.00	4.00	93.00
100.00	4.00	89.00

101.00	4.00	89.00
102.00	4.00	79.00
103.00	4.00	83.00
104.00	4.00	94.00
105.00	4.00	74.00
106.00	4.00	90.00
107.00	4.00	94.00
108.00	4.00	95.00
109.00	4.00	84.00
110.00	4.00	91.00
111.00	4.00	91.00
112.00	4.00	72.00
113.00	4.00	74.00
114.00	4.00	89.00
115.00	4.00	77.00
116.00	4.00	88.00
117.00	4.00	86.00
118.00	4.00	85.00
119.00	4.00	91.00
120.00	4.00	74.00

One-Way ANOVA: The Command

We can analyze the data from this One-way between-participants ANOVA design using the pull-down menus or by writing the syntax for the command in the SPSS® syntax editor (the command file). The written command is as follows:

Syntax Command

ONE-WAY
grade BY living
/STATISTICS DESCRIPTIVES HOMOGENEITY

/MISSING ANALYSIS
/POSTHOC = LSD ALPHA(.01).

Where GRADE is the dependent variable and LIVING is the independent variable.

This syntax command will calculate the omnibus *F* statistic, will conduct a test of the assumption of homogeneity of variances, and will conduct *post hoc* multiple comparisons using Fisher's Least Significant Difference Test (LSD). The SPSS® default significance level for post hoc testing is a=.05, but we need to change this to a=.01. We make this change by listing .01 parenthetically after we request the Fisher's LSD *post hoc* test. This command will also calculate the means and standard deviations for each of the treatment groups.

Menu Commands

The pull-down menu may also be used to analysis the data from the "Statistics" menu in the task bar. Select the "Compare Means" item and then the "One-way ANOVA." (See Figure 3.1) The One-way window will open. Now highlight the dependent variable name (GRADE) and then click on the black arrow between the variable list window (the window with all of the variable names listed) and the "dependent" window.

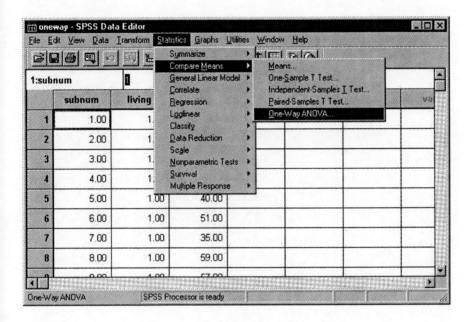

Figure 3.1: One-Way Menu Command

Next you need to select the independent variable or "factor." So, highlight the independent variable name (LIVING) and click on the black arrow next to the "factor" window. Now we have identified the independent and dependent variables in our research design.

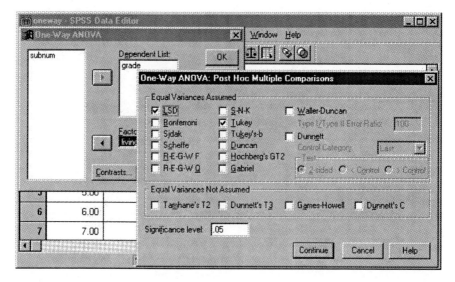

Figure 3.2: One-Way Post Hoc Tests

After we identify the research variables in this One-way ANOVA window, we must request multiple comparison tests. So click on the "post hoc" button in the One-way window. You can select any of 14 multiple comparison tests, but the three (3) most commonly used are Fisher's Least Significant Difference (LSD) test, Tukey's Honestly significant Difference (HSD) test, or the Student-Newman-Keuls (S-N-K) test (See Figure 3.2). The LSD is the least stringent (or easiest to find significant differences between treatments), the HSD test is most stringent, and the S-N-K is moderately stringent. After, selecting the post hoc multiple comparison test you will use, then click on the "Continue" button at the bottom of the "Post Hoc" window. Next, click on the "Options" button at the bottom of the "One-way ANOVA" window. You should select both of the options under the "Statistics" option, "Descriptives" and "Homogeneity-of-variance." The "descriptives" option will calculate the means and standard deviations for each of our 4 treatment conditions and the "Homogeneity" option will calculate Levene's test for the equality of variances (a test of the assumptions that all 4 populations variances are equal to each other: $s_1^2=s_2^2=s_3^2=s_4^2$). Now you are ready to run the One-way command by clicking the "OK" button on the right-hand side of the "One-way ANOVA" window.

>Statistics
> Compare Means
>One-way ANOVA
>[identify the independent variable (Factor) and the dependent variable from the variable list on the left of the window]
>Post Hoc
    >[select desired multiple comparison test(s)]
>Options
    >Descriptives
    >Homogeneity-of-variances
>OK

One-Way ANOVA: Interpreting the Results

Descriptives Table

The output file of the One-way command lists four tables. The first table is the One-way descriptives table (See Figure 3.3). This table lists the means and standard deviations of each treatment condition in the research design. This information is important because when you report the results of the One-way research design in a research report, you must include the mean and standard deviation of each treatment group, regardless of whether there were significant differences between the groups or not.

Homogeneity of Variance Table

The next table was generated when you requested the "Homogeneity" selection from the "Options" menu. This lists Levene's statistic for the test of homogeneity of variances between the treatment populations. To evaluate Levene's test, compare the value listed under "Sig." in this table to our decision rule of .01 (or whatever decision rule you are using to evaluate the One-way F statistic). Since the output shows that Levene's statistic has a significance level of .552 for this chapter example, we *have not* broken the assumption of homogeneity and can continue with the evaluation of the One-way F statistic. If the value of the significance level listed next to Levene's test is equal to or less than the decision rule (a=.01) then we must make an adjustment to the Within-Groups (Error) degrees of freedom for the F statistic. We simply multiple Levene's statistic by the Within-Groups degrees of freedom listed in the source table below the Homogeneity table. This adjustment will lower the error degrees of freedom.

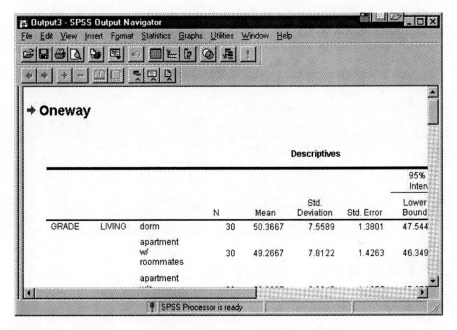

Figure 3.3: Descriptives Table

Then we would use a table for critical values of *F* to evaluate the *F* statistic with the adjusted error degrees of freedom.

Source Table

The next table listed in the One-way ANOVA print-out is called the ANOVA source table (See Figure 3.4). This lists the sources of variation as between groups (or treatment variance), within groups (or error variance), and total variance. The sum of squares, degrees of freedom (df), mean squares, *F* statistic, and the significance level of the *F* statistic. To evaluate the statistical significance of this *F* statistic we examine the "Sig." value printed in the source table. The "Sig." value listed is .000, which we interpret as $p < .001$. Since this is less than our decision rule of a=.01, we would "Reject the H_0" and conclude that there is a significant difference between at least two of the treatment population means.

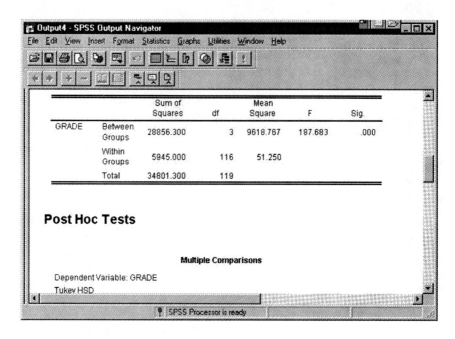

Figure 3.4: One-Way ANOVA Source Table

Post Hoc Multiple Comparison Tests

The next step is to evaluate the *post hoc* multiple comparison test results to determine which means are significantly different from each other. SPSS® lists all of the possible pairwise (or two group) comparisons twice. Each treatment group is listed under group "I" and "J" in the multiple comparisons table. SPSS® calculates the "Mean Difference" listed in this table by taking the treatment mean of the first group (group "I") and subtracting the treatment mean of the second group (group "J"). To determine if the comparison is statistically significant, we compare the "Sig." level listed for each unique *post hoc* test to our decision rule (a=.01). As we examine the multiple comparisons table we see that all 3 of the comparisons involving the LIVING SITUATION of "Living with Parents" are significant (all 3 significance levels listed are .000, which we interpret as .001). Now we need to determine which of the treatment means was greater in value for these 3 significant comparisons. We do this be examining the "Mean Difference" listed for each comparison test. The mean differences between "Living with Parents" and "Dorm" (35.33), "Living with Parents" and "Apartment with Roommates" (36.43), and "Living with Parents" and "Apartment without Roommates" (35.63) are all positive values. This means that the treatment group listed under "I" had a significantly greater course grade percentage (the dependent variable) than the treatment group listed under group "J."

When you report the F statistic and/or the multiple comparisons, it should take the following format. This would be reported in the Results section of an APA style research manuscript:

Results of the One-way ANOVA showed that the overall F was significant, $F(3,116) = 187.68$, $MS_E = 51.25$, $p < .001$. Post hoc comparisons, conducted using Fisher's LSD, relieved that those students who lived with their parents ($M = 85.7$, $SD = 6.78$) performed significantly better in the statistics course than those who lived in a dorm ($M = 50.37$, $SD = 7.56$), those who lived in an apartment with roommates ($M = 49.27$, $SD = 7.81$), those who lived in an apartment without roommates ($M = 50.07$, $SD = 6.4$).

Notice that the means (M) and standard deviations (SD) are reported immediately after each treatment condition is mentioned in the research conclusion. Also notice that reporting results of an ANOVA always follows the form above: F followed by both treatment and error degrees of freedom ($df_{TX}=3$ and $df_E=116$) followed by the mean square error ($MS_E=51.25$) followed by the calculated significance level ($p < .001$).

Important point!

Remember that we only evaluate the *post hoc* multiple comparison when the overall *F* statistic is significant (i.e., has a significance level equal to or less than .01). If we evaluated the multiple comparisons after determining that the overall *F* statistic was nonsignificant, we run the risk of committing a Type I Error. If the overall *F* statistic was nonsignificant that would mean that we Failed to Reject the H_0 or that we retain the null hypothesis that states $m_1 = m_2 = m_3 = m_4$. So, if we are concluding that the null should be retained, there is no reason to continue to conduct statistical testing on the same data. When we make the statistical decision of "Fail to Reject H_0" we are concluding that the population means are equal, so we don't go searching for significant differences between pairs of treatment means. Even though we request *post hoc* multiple comparisons prior to conducting the overall ANOVA (we get the results of the overall *F* and the multiple comparisons tests at the same time), we only evaluate the multiple comparisons when the *F* statistic is significant.

One-Way ANOVA: Further Practice

Let's study the effects of alcohol on driving ability. We design a study that involves three (3) levels of ALCOHOL CONSUMPTION (the independent variable): (1) No alcohol; (2) 24 oz of beer; and (3) 48 oz of beer consumed in 60 minutes. The dependent variable will be DRIVING ABILITY, which we can measure on a closed-circuit driving course that uses orange construction cones as the course boundaries. The dependent variable will be measured as the number of cones hit by the driver, so lower dependent variable values represent better driving ability and higher values represent worse driving ability. Using the following data, conduct the One-way ANOVA and write up the results section of an APA manuscript based on your analysis. Write up the results of this One-Way ANOVA in APA format and style in a typical Results section.

SUBNUM	ALCOHOL	DRIVING
1.00	1.00	6.00
2.00	1.00	9.00
3.00	1.00	10.00
4.00	1.00	7.00
5.00	1.00	8.00
6.00	1.00	6.00
7.00	1.00	8.00
8.00	1.00	9.00
9.00	1.00	6.00
10.00	1.00	9.00
11.00	1.00	7.00
12.00	1.00	8.00
13.00	1.00	9.00
14.00	1.00	6.00
15.00	1.00	7.00
16.00	1.00	7.00
17.00	1.00	7.00
18.00	1.00	8.00
19.00	1.00	7.00
20.00	1.00	9.00
21.00	1.00	8.00
22.00	1.00	8.00
23.00	1.00	8.00
24.00	1.00	8.00
25.00	1.00	8.00
26.00	1.00	8.00

27.00	1.00	10.00
28.00	1.00	7.00
29.00	1.00	9.00
30.00	1.00	8.00
31.00	2.00	3.00
32.00	2.00	4.00
33.00	2.00	3.00
34.00	2.00	2.00
35.00	2.00	3.00
36.00	2.00	7.00
37.00	2.00	2.00
38.00	2.00	3.00
39.00	2.00	5.00
40.00	2.00	2.00
41.00	2.00	3.00
42.00	2.00	5.00
43.00	2.00	3.00
44.00	2.00	4.00
45.00	2.00	4.00
46.00	2.00	3.00
47.00	2.00	2.00
48.00	2.00	6.00
49.00	2.00	7.00
50.00	2.00	2.00
51.00	2.00	6.00
52.00	2.00	7.00
53.00	2.00	5.00
54.00	2.00	4.00
55.00	2.00	5.00
56.00	2.00	2.00
57.00	2.00	5.00
58.00	2.00	5.00

59.00	2.00	4.00
60.00	2.00	5.00
61.00	3.00	3.00
62.00	3.00	5.00
63.00	3.00	4.00
64.00	3.00	5.00
65.00	3.00	3.00
66.00	3.00	4.00
67.00	3.00	6.00
68.00	3.00	5.00
69.00	3.00	5.00
70.00	3.00	5.00
71.00	3.00	6.00
72.00	3.00	7.00
73.00	3.00	5.00
74.00	3.00	6.00
75.00	3.00	5.00
76.00	3.00	3.00
77.00	3.00	5.00
78.00	3.00	2.00
79.00	3.00	4.00
80.00	3.00	4.00
81.00	3.00	4.00
82.00	3.00	5.00
83.00	3.00	4.00
84.00	3.00	4.00
85.00	3.00	5.00
86.00	3.00	4.00
87.00	3.00	3.00
88.00	3.00	2.00
89.00	3.00	5.00
90.00	3.00	7.00

Chapter 4: Factorial Analysis of Variance

Factorial ANOVA: The Research Question

Good news! We received a federal grant to continue our groundbreaking research on the effect of green M&Ms on sexual desire. However, this time we have proposed a between subjects factorial design because we would also like to examine whether gender of participants plays a role. So, in our grant proposal we specified a 2 X 2 between subjects factorial design with two levels of M&M color (green=1 and red=2) and two levels of participants' gender (1=female and 2=male). We will again operationalize our dependent variable by the Horniness Scale which has a range of scores from 1 (not at all horny) to 10 (very horny). We will use a post hoc comparison (multiple comparison) test to determine if any simple main effects exist. That is to say, we will use Fisher's LSD test.

Factorial ANOVA: The Data

We should use 120 total subjects because that would mean there were 30 participants in each treatment group (2 x 2 Factorial has 4 treatment groups), so the Central Limit Theorem is in effect. For the sake of ease, we only used a total of 60 subjects. You could appreciate how long a list of 120 participants would be! Remember that there are two levels of M&M color (green=1 and red=2) and two levels of participants' gender (1=female and 2=male). The dependent variable is HORNY and ranges from 1 to 20. Don't forget to label everything once you have your data file complete.

SUBNUM	MandM	GENDER	HORNY
1.00	1.00	1.00	8.00
2.00	1.00	1.00	10.00
3.00	1.00	1.00	9.00
4.00	1.00	1.00	9.00
5.00	1.00	1.00	8.00
6.00	1.00	1.00	7.00
7.00	1.00	1.00	10.00
8.00	1.00	1.00	8.00
9.00	1.00	1.00	9.00
10.00	1.00	1.00	7.00
11.00	1.00	1.00	9.00
12.00	1.00	1.00	8.00
13.00	1.00	1.00	6.00
14.00	1.00	1.00	8.00
15.00	1.00	1.00	10.00
16.00	1.00	2.00	4.00
17.00	1.00	2.00	5.00
18.00	1.00	2.00	3.00
19.00	1.00	2.00	2.00
20.00	1.00	2.00	3.00
21.00	1.00	2.00	3.00
22.00	1.00	2.00	7.00
23.00	1.00	2.00	4.00
24.00	1.00	2.00	5.00
25.00	1.00	2.00	4.00
26.00	1.00	2.00	5.00
27.00	1.00	2.00	5.00
28.00	1.00	2.00	4.00
29.00	1.00	2.00	6.00
30.00	1.00	2.00	4.00
31.00	2.00	1.00	2.00

32.00	2.00	1.00	4.00
33.00	2.00	1.00	5.00
34.00	2.00	1.00	6.00
35.00	2.00	1.00	5.00
36.00	2.00	1.00	3.00
37.00	2.00	1.00	4.00
38.00	2.00	1.00	6.00
39.00	2.00	1.00	5.00
40.00	2.00	1.00	4.00
41.00	2.00	1.00	4.00
42.00	2.00	1.00	5.00
43.00	2.00	1.00	4.00
44.00	2.00	1.00	4.00
45.00	2.00	1.00	7.00
46.00	2.00	2.00	4.00
47.00	2.00	2.00	3.00
48.00	2.00	2.00	4.00
49.00	2.00	2.00	6.00
50.00	2.00	2.00	4.00
51.00	2.00	2.00	2.00
52.00	2.00	2.00	4.00
53.00	2.00	2.00	4.00
54.00	2.00	2.00	5.00
55.00	2.00	2.00	2.00
56.00	2.00	2.00	5.00
57.00	2.00	2.00	5.00
58.00	2.00	2.00	5.00
59.00	2.00	2.00	5.00
60.00	2.00	2.00	6.00

Factorial ANOVA: The Command

Syntax Command

Following is the simplest version of the written command. MANOVA stands for Multivariate Analysis of Variance and is typically used when we have designs which use two or more factors and two or more dependent variables. Those are complicated designs that I will not discuss here. Wait until you go to graduate school! But the command is useful for us when we are analyzing a factorial design because it allows us to request cell means for later use during our multiple comparisons. So here's the command.

```
MANOVA horny by mandm(1,2) gender(1,2)
/PRINT SIGNIF(AVONLY)
/OMEANS.
```

Where HORNY is the dependent variable, and MANDM and GENDER are the two factors, with the minimum and maximum values for those variables. The next two command lines produce a table of cell means and a source table. I always teach my students to run a factorial using this command because it provides you with two tables that are easy to read and helpful. The first table is of cell means and the second is the source table.

Menu Command

Using the pull-down menus (See Figure 4.1), you need to click on 'Statistics,' 'General Linear Model,' and then 'GLM—General Factorial.' This will open the 'General Factorial' window. The first variable to identify is the dependent variable by clicking on the variable name to the left and then clicking on the black arrow next to the 'Dependent Variable' box (See Figure 4.2). The next variables you will need to identify are the independent variables (or factors).

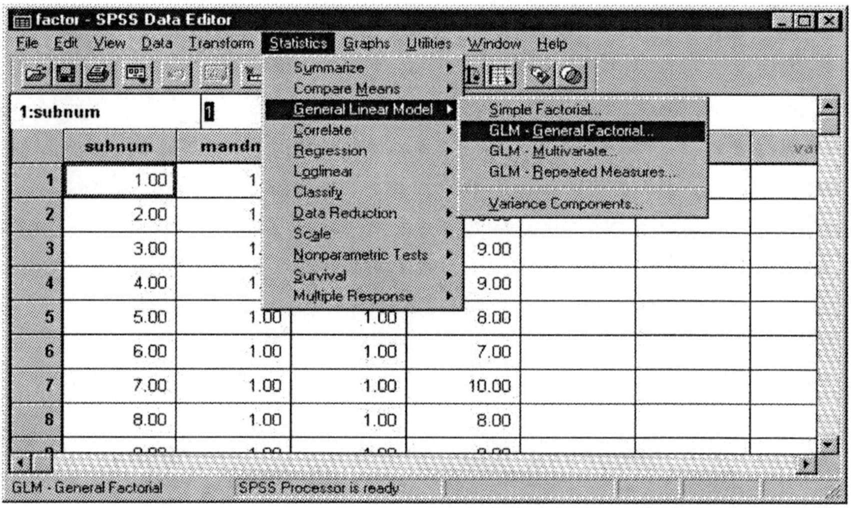

Figure 4.1: Selecting the General Factorial Procedure

Most of the time you will have a fixed ANOVA model. This is when you are interested in studying the effects of the specific (or fixed) levels of the factor. We picked green and red M&M® color because we were interested in a comparison of these specific colors, not any others. There are other research questions that would be appropriately analyzed using the random effects model. For example, a drug researcher may be interested in determining the dose of a drug necessary to effect an particular ailment. If the researcher does not have a clear idea of the necessary dosage, then a random effects model would be used to randomly select dosing levels. While some research questions are necessarily analyzed using the random effects model, most research studies are designed to test the effects of specific levels of the independent variable (i.e., factor).

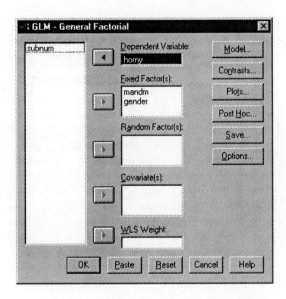

Figure 4.2: Identifying Variables for the Factorial Design

We can also identify a covariate to include in the analysis. Covariates are continuously measured variables that the researcher believes are related to the dependent variable. In our research design, we might think that age would be related to horniness, so we could use age as a covariate. The 'Options' button allows us to request 'Descriptives statistics' and 'Homogeneity tests' for our design (See Figure 4.3).

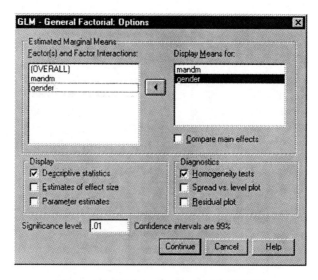

Figure 4.3: Options for Factorial ANOVA

There are a few options that you can choose to display like 'Descriptive statistics,' 'Estimates of effect size,' and 'Homogeneity tests.' These options will allow you to more fully understand what's going on with your data.

Once you have identified the dependent variable, the factors, and any covariates, you can paste the command if you want to print it or save it. You can run the command simply by clicking on the 'OK' button.

>Statistics
>General Linear Model
>GLM—General Factorial
>[Identify the "Dependent Variable"]
>[Identify the "Fixed Factors"]
>[Identify "Covariates"]
>Options

>Descriptives statistics
>Homogeneity tests
>Continue
>OK

Factorial ANOVA: Interpreting the Results

The print-out contains a series of tables. The first table lists the number of valid observations for this research, followed by the second table that displays the cell means.

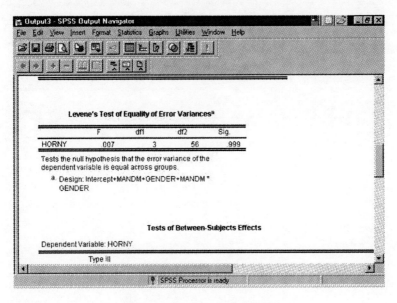

Figure 4.4: Levene's Test Table

In the third table are the results of Levene's test for the equality of variances, otherwise known as homogeneity of variance (See Figure 4.4). For our data, Levene's test shows that we have not broken this assumption because the 'Sig.' calculated for the F (3,56)=.007 was .999, which is larger than our decision rule of .01. The final table is the source table (See Figure 4.5). Along the left-hand side of the table are the 'Source of Variation' being tested. Moving to the right across the table are the sum of squares ('SS'), degrees of freedom ('df'), mean squares ('MS'), and the F statistic and its significance level. Since we also requested effect size, we have Eta Squared, which tells us the proportion of total variability attributable to each of the sources of variation in our study. SPSS® has also calculated the power of the statistical tests conducted for this analysis.

```
Output3 - SPSS Output Navigator
File  Edit  View  Insert  Format  Statistics  Graphs  Utilities  Window  Help
```

Tests of Between-Subjects Effects

Dependent Variable: HORNY

Source	Type III Sum of Squares	df	Mean Square	F	Sig.	Noncent. Parameter	Observed Power[a]
Corrected Model	184.733[b]	3	61.578	40.474	.000	121.421	1.000
Intercept	1728.067	1	1728.067	1135.818	.000	1135.818	1.000
MANDM	56.067	1	56.067	36.851	.000	36.851	1.000
GENDER	72.600	1	72.600	47.718	.000	47.718	1.000
MANDM * GENDER	56.067	1	56.067	36.851	.000	36.851	1.000
Error	85.200	56	1.521				
Total	1998.000	60					
Corrected Total	269.933	59					

SPSS Processor is ready

Figure 4.5: ANOVA Source Table

Remember that to determine if a main effect or the interaction is significant, we compare the 'Sig of F' to our decision rule (a=.01). If the printed significance level is less than or equal to our decision rule then we will reject that H_0 and conclude the effect is statistically significant. If the significance level is greater than a, then we fail to reject the H_0, which means the effect was non-significant.

Just a couple of things you should notice about the numbers in the table. Notice that the sum of squares for the M&M main effect plus the GENDER main effect plus the interaction add up to the sum of squares listed for the 'Corrected Model.' Corrected Model is another way of saying total treatment sum of squares. So, if we add up all of the sum of squares for the treatment effects (i.e., the interaction and two main effects) and the error term, we will get a result equal to the 'Correct Model' sum of squares. In analysis of variance we partition the variance in the design. The degrees of freedom are handled the same way. The total 'DF' can be partitioned into the error degrees of freedom and the treatment degrees of freedom. Our interaction $(df_{M\&MxGender}=df_{M\&M}Xdf_{Gender})$ and two main effects $(df_{M\&M}=k-1; df_{Gender}=k-1)$ have df=1 and the error degrees of freedom are 56 $(df_{Error}=N-K)$, which equals the corrected model total degrees of freedom (df_T) = 59.

There are five *F*s listed in the output file. If you haven't stated specific research hypotheses involving the main effects, then we first interpret the interaction term. So look first at the F and Sig of F for the 'GENDER*MANDM' interaction term. If this is significant, then we would examine the design for simple main effects (or comparisons between cells) using a multiple comparison test like LSD. If the interaction is significant that means that one factor moderates the effect that the other factor has on the dependent variable. If the interaction is non-significant, we examine both main effects for M&M and GENDER. If either of these are significant, then we compare the group means (since there are only two levels of both of these factors) to determine which group scored higher on the HORNY scale.

In our example we wouldn't have to conduct multiple comparisons (for the significant main effects) because we only have two levels of the factor, so we know which levels are significantly different. In the Further Practice section you will be faced with a 2 X 3 factorial design. If the interaction or the main effect for the second factor (with three levels) is significant, you will have to conduct multiple comparisons.

When you report the F statistic and/or the multiple comparisons, it should take the following format:

Research examining the effect of M&Ms on horniness showed that male participants who ate the green M&Ms (M=8.40,SD=.97) reported significantly more horniness than either females who ate green M&Ms (M=4.20,SD=1.75) or males who ate red M&Ms(M=5.10,SD=1.20) [F$(1,36) = 17.99$, $MS_E = 1.70$, $p < .001$].

Factorial ANOVA: Further Practice

You are a social psychologist researching the effect that mode of transmission (MOT) and gender of patient has on attributions of blame toward people who are HIV positive. You decide to use a 2x3 between subjects factorial design. Gender (1=females; 2=males) and mode of transmission (1=male/male sexual activity; 2=female/male sexual activity; 3=unknown mode) are thought to have an interaction effect on attributions of blame (1=no blame; 100=extreme blame) for the patient. Using the following data, run the factorial analysis and write up the results in APA style.

SUBNUM	GENDER	MOT	BLAME
1.00	1.00	1.00	75.00
2.00	1.00	1.00	76.00
3.00	1.00	1.00	91.00
4.00	1.00	1.00	78.00
5.00	1.00	1.00	84.00
6.00	1.00	1.00	70.00
7.00	1.00	1.00	80.00

8.00	1.00	1.00	96.00
9.00	1.00	1.00	77.00
10.00	1.00	1.00	81.00
11.00	1.00	2.00	53.00
12.00	1.00	2.00	51.00
13.00	1.00	2.00	46.00
14.00	1.00	2.00	63.00
15.00	1.00	2.00	58.00
16.00	1.00	2.00	57.00
17.00	1.00	2.00	43.00
18.00	1.00	2.00	51.00
19.00	1.00	2.00	54.00
20.00	1.00	2.00	61.00
21.00	1.00	3.00	52.00
22.00	1.00	3.00	53.00
23.00	1.00	3.00	36.00
24.00	1.00	3.00	55.00
25.00	1.00	3.00	52.00
26.00	1.00	3.00	55.00
27.00	1.00	3.00	54.00
28.00	1.00	3.00	41.00
29.00	1.00	3.00	49.00
30.00	1.00	3.00	48.00
31.00	2.00	1.00	52.00
32.00	2.00	1.00	49.00
33.00	2.00	1.00	39.00
34.00	2.00	1.00	38.00
35.00	2.00	1.00	44.00
36.00	2.00	1.00	49.00
37.00	2.00	1.00	47.00
38.00	2.00	1.00	57.00
39.00	2.00	1.00	48.00

40.00	2.00	1.00	53.00
41.00	2.00	2.00	44.00
42.00	2.00	2.00	54.00
43.00	2.00	2.00	34.00
44.00	2.00	2.00	53.00
45.00	2.00	2.00	49.00
46.00	2.00	2.00	48.00
47.00	2.00	2.00	50.00
48.00	2.00	2.00	41.00
49.00	2.00	2.00	54.00
50.00	2.00	2.00	48.00
51.00	2.00	3.00	52.00
52.00	2.00	3.00	53.00
53.00	2.00	3.00	32.00
54.00	2.00	3.00	53.00
55.00	2.00	3.00	40.00
56.00	2.00	3.00	47.00
57.00	2.00	3.00	44.00
58.00	2.00	3.00	39.00
59.00	2.00	3.00	55.00
60.00	2.00	3.00	39.00

Chapter 5: One-way Repeated Measures Analysis of Variance

One-Way Repeated Measures ANOVA: The Research Question

Now let's consider a research design that involves the repeated measurement of the same sample of study participants over three or more measurement periods. These designs are called by a couple of different names including within-subject designs, within-participant designs, and repeated measures designs. Since the science of psychology is eliminating the use of the word "subjects" from is rubric, we will use the more accurate name of repeated measures. Make sure that you notice that SPSS® still employs the more archaic phrase "within-subjects" throughout the repeated measure ANOVA procedure. These designs involve multiple measurement of the same sample of people across the different treatment conditions. As we learned in Chapter 3, between-participant designs involve a separate sample of participants for each treatment condition. When we utilize a repeated measures design, we select only one sample of study participants and they experience all of the treatment conditions (i.e., all of the levels of the independent variable).

For this chapter, let's examine the effect of multiple viewing of a cartoon on the ratings of humor for a group of 7 year old children. We will show a sample of 30 children the same cartoon three (3) times (the independent variable: VIEWING) and then ask them to rate the humor of the cartoon (the dependent variable: HUMOR). We'll measure the children's ratings of humor on a 1=not at all funny to 10=very funny. When conducting this type of research involving ratings of a variable by young children, it is common to use a graphic response scale from a smiling face to a frowning face.

One-Way Repeated Measures ANOVA: The Data

Following is the data we have collected for the One-way repeated measures design. Remember that in repeated measures designs, every participant experiences all of the treatment conditions. So, each of the values listed under the three VIEW conditions are ratings of humor (the dependent variable measure).

SUBNUM	VIEW1	VIEW2	VIEW3
1.00	7.00	6.00	3.00
2.00	8.00	5.00	4.00
3.00	9.00	2.00	5.00
4.00	7.00	6.00	6.00
5.00	6.00	4.00	4.00
6.00	7.00	5.00	2.00
7.00	7.00	4.00	3.00
8.00	7.00	4.00	4.00
9.00	8.00	4.00	5.00
10.00	10.00	7.00	5.00
11.00	8.00	7.00	5.00
12.00	8.00	4.00	3.00
13.00	8.00	3.00	5.00
14.00	6.00	4.00	6.00
15.00	8.00	3.00	2.00
16.00	8.00	6.00	4.00
17.00	10.00	6.00	3.00
18.00	9.00	4.00	6.00
19.00	7.00	5.00	5.00
20.00	7.00	3.00	5.00
21.00	9.00	4.00	6.00

22.00	9.00	4.00	5.00
23.00	8.00	6.00	5.00
24.00	10.00	7.00	6.00
25.00	8.00	3.00	5.00
26.00	9.00	5.00	5.00
27.00	9.00	3.00	5.00
28.00	8.00	5.00	4.00
29.00	6.00	5.00	6.00
30.00	10.00	6.00	2.00

One-Way Repeated Measures ANOVA: The Command

Syntax Command

Following is the syntax structure of the one-way repeated measures ANOVA. It was created using the menu command discussed below.

```
GLM
view1 view2 view3
/WSFACTOR = view 3 Polynomial
/METHOD = SSTYPE(3)
/EMMEANS = TABLES(view)
/PRINT = DESCRIPTIVE
/CRITERIA = ALPHA(.05)
/WSDESIGN = view .
```

Where VIEW1 VIEW2 VIEW3 are the three repeated measures of the dependent variable and "VIEW 3" in the ""WSFACTOR" subcommand is the name of the repeated measure variable and the number of levels. We could also use the pull down menus to analyze the data from this repeated measures ANOVA design. Notice that "view1," view2," and "view3" defined as variables in the SPSS® data file and syntax files, but in the research design these are three levels of the repeated measures factor (i.e., independent variable), which we defined in the "WSFACTORS" subcommand as VIEW. Make sure you understand the difference between an independent variable (or factor) and the levels of that factor.

Menu Command

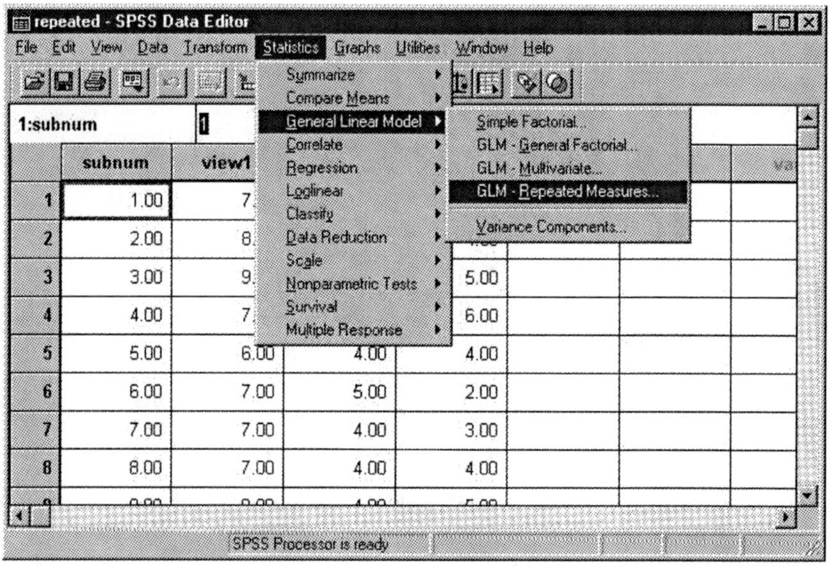

Figure 5.1: Selecting the GLM—Repeated Measures Option

For our example, enter the variable name VIEW for the repeated measures factor and enter 3 levels of the repeated measures factor. When selecting the levels of the repeated measures factor make sure that you select the levels in the correct order. You can do this easily by left clicking on the VIEW1 variable and drag the mouse down until VIEW2 and VIEW3 are highlighted. Once you have highlighted all three levels, click on the black arrow button to define the levels of the VIEW factor (See Figure 5.2).

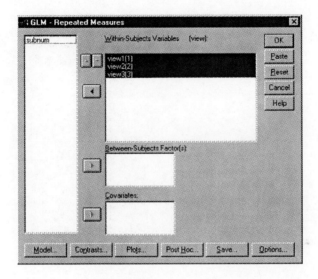

Figure 5.2: Repeated Measures ANOVA Window

Next, click on the "Options" button. When we request the "Descriptive statistics" option we need to first select the factor VIEW from the "Factor(s) and Factor Interactions" windowpane (See Figure 5.3). Click on "Continue" and then finally, click on "OK" and SPSS® does the rest!

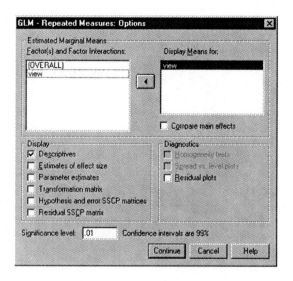

Figure 5.3: Repeated Measures Options: Descriptives

>Statistics
>General Linear Model
>Repeated Measures
      >[Enter name of repeated measures factor]
      >[Enter number of levels of repeated measures factor]
      >Define
>[Select the levels of the repeated measures factor from the variable list]
   >Options
      >[Select repeated measures factor for "Display Means for:"]
      >[Select "Descriptive statistics"]
      >Continue
   >OK

One-Way Repeated Measures ANOVA: Interpreting the Results

The output file for this analysis includes eight tables: (1) Within-Subjects Factor, which lists the levels of the repeated measures factor (i.e., within-subjects factor); (2) Descriptive Statistics, which listed the means and standard deviations for each of the repeated measures levels; (3) Multivariate Tests, which *we use only when the assumption of sphericity* has been broken; (4) Mauchly's Test of Sphericity, which we evaluate to determine if sphericity can be assumed; (5) Tests of Within-Subjects Effects that lists the results of our repeated measures ANOVA, under the assumption that sphericity has not been broken; (6) Tests of Within-Subjects Contrasts, which reports contracts between the first two and the third levels of the repeated measures factor; (7) Test of Between-Subjects Effects, which is a nonsense table when examining only a repeated measures factor (more specifically it tests the hypothesis that the average of the three treatment means is different than zero); and (8) Estimated Marginal Means for our repeated measures factor VIEW, which reports the means and standard error for each of the three levels of the VIEW factor. In order to interpret the output, we must first determine if we should assume sphericity or not.

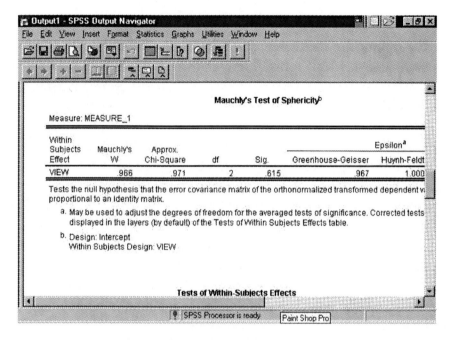

Figure 5.4: Mauchly's Test of Sphericity

The first table that we must examine is Mauchly's Test of Sphericity. Like all other statistics, we compare the significance levels of the statistical test (reported under "Sig." in the Mauchly table) to our decision rule (a=.01). In our study of watching the same cartoon and ratings of humor, *we have not broken the assumption of sphericity* (i.e., "Sig." = .615 > a = .01) (See Figure 5.4). Since we can assume sphericity, we will evaluate the *F* statistic list in the "Tests of Within-Subjects Effects" table, which immediately follows Mauchly's table in the output file.

This ANOVA source table (See Figure 5.5) reports variance estimates for the two sources of variability in our design: (1) treatment (VIEW) and (2) error. In addition to the variance estimates (or mean squares) of treatment and error, the source table also lists the sums of squares, degrees of freedom (df), the F ratio (i.e., statistic), and the significance level (Sig.) of the F test. This F statistic is significant because the calculated significance level for the statistic is $p < .001$ which is less than our decision rule of a=.01. The next step in the analysis would then be to conduct multiple comparison tests. Before we conduct these tests, let's examine how these numbers were calculated from the data. Remember that the F statistic, or sometime called the F ratio, is a ratio between variance due to the treatment conditions and variance due to error (unknown source(s) of variability). From the output then, our F statistic of 80.28 was calculated by dividing mean square treatment (MS_{VIEW}=120.48) by the mean square error (MS_{ERROR}=1.5). Working backward through the output, the mean squares were calculated by dividing the sums of squares by their respective degrees of freedom. So, the MS_{VIEW}=120.48 was calculated by dividing the SS_{VIEW}=240.96 by the df_{VIEW}=2. Likewise, the MS_{ERROR}=1.5 was calculated by dividing the SS_{ERROR}=87.04 by the df_{ERROR}=58. The df_{VIEW}=2 was calculated by the formula $df_{TREATMENT}$=k-1, where k=number of levels of the repeated measures factor. The df_{ERROR}=58 was calculated using the formula df_{ERROR}=($df_{TREATMENT}$) (n-1), where n=number of participants in the study. For our study then, the formula used was df_{ERROR} 2 x (30-1) = 58.

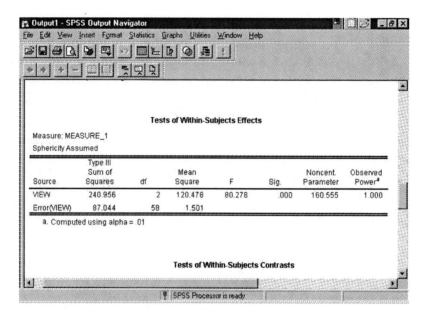

Figure 5.5: Repeated measure ANOVA Source Table

Notice that the Repeated Measures ANOVA command does not provide multiple comparison tests in the analysis. We must conduct these tests the old fashioned way, *by hand!* The formulae of most *post hoc* multiple comparison tests include the MS_{ERROR}, which we would get from the ANOVA source table. The df_{ERROR} is also needed for many of the *post hoc* tests and can also be found on this source table. The treatment means necessary for the multiple comparisons are reported in the first and last table of the repeated measures ANOVA output.

The "Tests of Between Subjects Effects" table is interpreted only when we are analyzing a split-plot ANOVA design (i.e., mixed designs). We will consider these designs in chapter 6. However, this "Between-Subjects" source table does report the calculated SS, df, and MS for the "Subjects" source of variation, which is listed in the row headed "Error."

If we divide the $MS_{ERROR} = 1.795$ from this table by the $MS_{ERROR}=1.501$ reported in the "Within-Subject" source table, we can test for order effects. In this case, we are specifically testing for order effects (i.e., repeated viewing of the same cartoon). But if we designed a study involving a repeated measures variable that may be open to order effects, we would want to statistically test for these effects. Of course, we would also use a counterbalancing scheme in the design of the research study in order to eliminate or reduce possible order effects. If we were to test for order effects in the study we conducted in this chapter, we would divide the $MS_{ERROR} = 1.795$ (from Between-Subjects table) by the $MS_{ERROR}=1.501$ (from Within-Subject table). In this fashion we would calculate the F ratio to test for order effects: $F_{ORDER\ EFFECTS} = 1.795/1/501 = 1.196$. Evaluating this F statistic using a=.01, $df_{SUBJECTS} = 8$ and $df_{ERROR} = 58$ ($F_{CV} » 4.95$) would lead us to the conclusion that this F statistic is nonsignificant, meaning that there were no order effects in this design. The final table ("Estimated Marginal Means") is simply a duplicate reporting of the treatment means in the first table.

One-way Repeated Measures ANOVA: Further Practice

Now we are interested in examining the effects of taking a statistics course on math anxiety. We will measure math anxiety on a (0=no anxiety;10=extremely high anxiety) scale on the first day of class, 4 weeks, 8 weeks, and 12 weeks into the semester. What do you conclude about the effects of taking a statistics course on the math anxiety of college students? Use Tukey's HSD for multiple comparisons and remember that you must conduct the multiple comparisons by hand. Remember that in SPSS® you must use variable names of 8 characters or less and that begin with a letter (try "FIRST," "WK4," "WK8," "WK12"). Report the results of this analysis in an APA style Results section.

STUDENT	FIRST DAY	4 WEEKS	8 WEEKS	12 WEEKS
1.00	5.00	5.00	6.00	8.00
2.00	3.00	4.00	3.00	10.00
3.00	3.00	3.00	6.00	9.00
4.00	4.00	4.00	3.00	9.00
5.00	5.00	5.00	4.00	10.00
6.00	5.00	5.00	4.00	9.00
7.00	4.00	5.00	5.00	8.00
8.00	2.00	5.00	5.00	8.00
9.00	4.00	2.00	7.00	9.00
10.00	5.00	4.00	6.00	10.00
11.00	3.00	7.00	4.00	8.00
12.00	3.00	5.00	4.00	9.00
13.00	6.00	3.00	6.00	7.00
14.00	3.00	4.00	4.00	10.00
15.00	6.00	6.00	6.00	8.00
16.00	2.00	3.00	3.00	8.00
17.00	5.00	2.00	5.00	8.00
18.00	4.00	3.00	2.00	9.00
19.00	6.00	6.00	6.00	7.00
20.00	4.00	6.00	5.00	10.00
21.00	4.00	5.00	4.00	8.00
22.00	3.00	3.00	4.00	9.00
23.00	3.00	6.00	5.00	7.00
24.00	5.00	4.00	3.00	7.00
25.00	2.00	5.00	6.00	6.00
26.00	5.00	3.00	5.00	9.00
27.00	5.00	3.00	4.00	10.00
28.00	3.00	4.00	4.00	10.00
29.00	5.00	6.00	4.00	7.00
30.00	5.00	2.00	3.00	8.00

Chapter 6: Split-plot Analysis of Variance

Split-plot ANOVA: The Research Question

For this chapter on using the analysis of variance for split-plot or mixed designs, we need to use one between-participants factor and one repeated measures factor. Let's examine the role that violence in video games has on children's aggressive behaviors. We design the study with an observational measure of aggressive behavior (our dependent variable) by counting the number of times an aggressive act, such as hitting, is observed from a group of children. Our two factors (or independent variables) will be the type of video game played (violent or non-violent) and a pretest-posttest-posttest measure. The pretest-posttest-posttest measure will be our repeated measures factor and the type of video game will be our between-participants factor.

Therefore, we have a 2 (type of video game) x 3 (pretest-posttest-posttest) split-plot design to test the effect of violence in video games on aggressive behavior in children. We will measure the dependent variable as a frequency of aggressive behavior which we would operational define prior to the study. For example, we might count as "aggressive" behaviors hitting another child, pushing or shoving another child, taking a toy that another child is playing with, etc. For the purposes of this example, let's say that the pretest and posttest observational periods are each 30 minutes long, with a possible range of dependent variable measures of 0-20. Let's also assume that we have a total of 30 children in each video game group (for a total N=60) and that the children are all the same age in years.

Split-plot ANOVA: The Data

We will have three measures of the dependent variable. The first measurement will take place before we allow the children to play the assigned video game, the second measurement will take place after the children have played their respective video games for one hour, and the third, and final, measurement will take place on the next day (to determine longer-term effects).

SUBNUM	GAME	PRETEST	POST1	POST2
1.00	1.00	7.00	9.00	15.00
2.00	1.00	5.00	9.00	17.00
3.00	1.00	12.00	10.00	16.00
4.00	1.00	8.00	10.00	16.00
5.00	1.00	11.00	10.00	17.00
6.00	1.00	8.00	7.00	16.00
7.00	1.00	13.00	10.00	14.00
8.00	1.00	7.00	8.00	18.00
9.00	1.00	8.00	10.00	15.00
10.00	1.00	6.00	7.00	14.00
11.00	1.00	12.00	11.00	14.00
12.00	1.00	7.00	11.00	16.00
13.00	1.00	11.00	8.00	15.00
14.00	1.00	12.00	12.00	17.00
15.00	1.00	10.00	8.00	15.00
16.00	1.00	8.00	8.00	12.00
17.00	1.00	12.00	9.00	16.00
18.00	1.00	9.00	6.00	14.00
19.00	1.00	6.00	11.00	20.00
20.00	1.00	7.00	8.00	16.00
21.00	1.00	7.00	8.00	20.00
22.00	1.00	7.00	10.00	14.00

23.00	1.00	9.00	13.00	15.00
24.00	1.00	10.00	11.00	18.00
25.00	1.00	11.00	8.00	18.00
26.00	1.00	10.00	7.00	20.00
27.00	1.00	11.00	7.00	15.00
28.00	1.00	12.00	12.00	19.00
29.00	1.00	8.00	11.00	16.00
30.00	1.00	12.00	10.00	14.00
31.00	2.00	9.00	7.00	6.00
32.00	2.00	5.00	9.00	10.00
33.00	2.00	9.00	10.00	8.00
34.00	2.00	8.00	8.00	11.00
35.00	2.00	8.00	8.00	7.00
36.00	2.00	12.00	11.00	10.00
37.00	2.00	7.00	6.00	11.00
38.00	2.00	12.00	9.00	13.00
39.00	2.00	9.00	6.00	9.00
40.00	2.00	10.00	12.00	12.00
41.00	2.00	11.00	8.00	12.00
42.00	2.00	7.00	11.00	7.00
43.00	2.00	11.00	6.00	6.00
44.00	2.00	8.00	7.00	5.00
45.00	2.00	9.00	10.00	8.00
46.00	2.00	6.00	8.00	10.00
47.00	2.00	12.00	9.00	10.00
48.00	2.00	9.00	9.00	11.00
49.00	2.00	12.00	7.00	9.00
50.00	2.00	7.00	9.00	6.00
51.00	2.00	10.00	11.00	5.00
52.00	2.00	6.00	10.00	8.00
53.00	2.00	8.00	9.00	9.00
54.00	2.00	12.00	12.00	6.00

55.00	2.00	9.00	6.00	6.00
56.00	2.00	14.00	6.00	9.00
57.00	2.00	10.00	7.00	8.00
58.00	2.00	10.00	6.00	9.00
59.00	2.00	12.00	8.00	10.00
60.00	2.00	7.00	8.00	10.00

Split-plot ANOVA: The Command

Syntax Command

Following is syntax command to analysis the 2 x 3 split-plot design using the general linear model—repeated measures command.

```
GLM
pre post1 post2 BY game
/WSFACTOR = test 3 Polynomial
/METHOD = SSTYPE(3)
/EMMEANS = TABLES(game*test)
/EMMEANS = TABLES(test)
/EMMEANS = TABLES(game)
/PRINT = DESCRIPTIVE HOMOGENEITY
/CRITERIA = ALPHA(.01)
/WSDESIGN = test
/DESIGN = game .
```

Where PRE, POST1, and POST2 and GAME are variable names in the data file. Remember that even though SPSS® treats PRE, POST1, and POST2 as variables, they are levels of the factor we identified as TEST in the "WSFACTOR" subcommand. Also notice that we identify the number of levels of the within-participant factor when we identify "3" after the factor name.

Menu Command

To use the pull-down menus we again click on the "Statistics" option in the word menu at the top of the SPSS® data file. Next, we highlight "General Linear Model" and then the "GLM—Repeated Measures" option (See Figure 6.1). This will open the "GLM—Repeated Measures Define Factor(s)" window (See Figure 6.2).

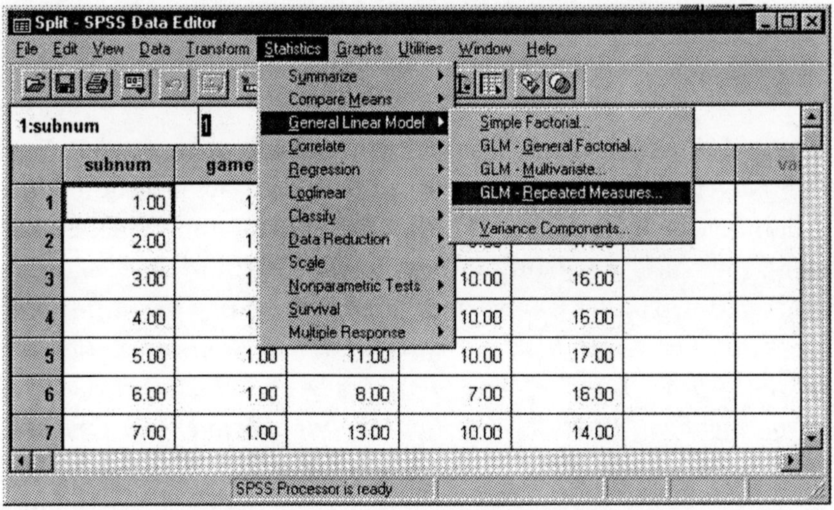

Figure 6.1: Selecting the GLM-Repeated Measures Procedure

Let's call our within-participant factor TEST by typing test in the windowpane next to "Within-Subject Factor Name." Next, we need to define the number of levels that our within-participant factor has in our design, so type the number "3" in the "Number of Levels" window-pane and click on the "Add" button. Once we have identified the name and levels of the within-participant factor we can define the research design by clicking on the "Define" button (See Figure 6.2).

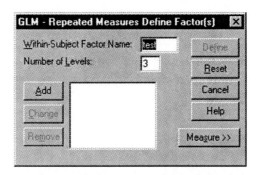

Figure 6.2: Define Factor(s) Window

The "GLM—Repeated Measures" window will open up (See Figure 6.3). First, let's define the three levels of the TEST factor by individually highlighting the level names: (1) PRE; (2) POST1; and (3) POST2 and clicking the black arrow button next to the "Within-Subjects Variable (test)" windowpane. *It is important to note two things about this procedure: (1) that you must highlight and click the black arrow button in the order that you want the repeated measures levels to be reported, and (2) that you highlight the levels name and then immediately click the arrow button.* Next, we will identify the between-participant factor by highlighting the GAME variable name and clicking the black arrow button next to the "Between-Subjects Factor(s)" windowpane (See Figure 6.3).

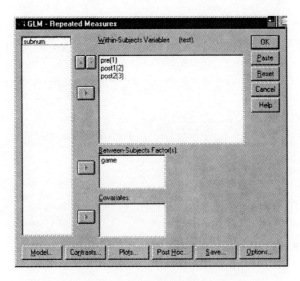

Figure 6.3: Repeated Measures Window

Since we have no covariates in the design, we are done identifying the variables involved in this study. Remember that a covariate is a continuously measured variable that we believe is significantly related to the dependent variable and may interact with the two factors in our design. A possible covariate for our example design in this chapter could have been the emotional maturity of the children in the study as measured by one of a number of available tests.

We can also request that other statistics be computed for us by clicking the "Options" button. At a minimum you will probably want to request "Descriptives" and "Homogeneity tests" (See Figure 6.4). When you select "Descriptives," you must also double-click on both the TEST and GAME factor names. This will provide a print-out that lists the means and standard deviations for each of our 6 treatment conditions. After selecting the "Descriptives" and "Homogeneity tests" options, click on the "Continue" button and then the "OK" button in the "GLM—Repeated Measures" window.

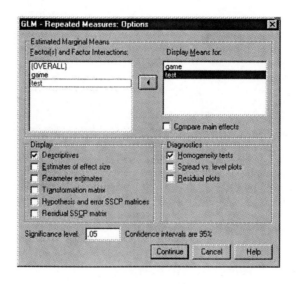

Figure 6.4: Selecting Descriptives and Homogeneity Tests in the Repeated Measures Options Window

Split-plot ANOVA: Interpreting the Results

The results of the split-plot ANOVA are reported in 12 separate tables. The first 2 tables simply list the names and levels of the two factors in the design (the Within-Subjects Factors and Between-Subjects Factors). The next table lists the "Descriptive Statistics" for each of our 6 treatment cells. Of course, these descriptives are necessary for any multiple comparison testing as well as for reporting our results in an APA style research manuscript. The next table (i.e., "Box's Test of Equality of Covariance Matrices") is unnecessary for the current design because we have only one dependent variable (that is, we are conducting univariate statistics).

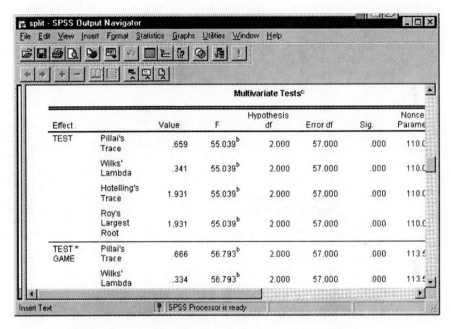

Figure 6.5: Multivariate Test Results in the SPSS® Output File

The fifth table is the list of "Multivariate Tests" for the split-plot ANOVA (See Figure 6.5). However, to decide if we will interpret these ANOVA results we must first determine if we can assume sphericity. The sixth table lists the results of the "Mauchly's Test of Sphericity" (See Figure 6.6). In our example, the "Sig." (or significance level of the Mauchly's W statistic) is calculated as .461, which means that we can assume sphericity (we have not broken the sphericity assumption).

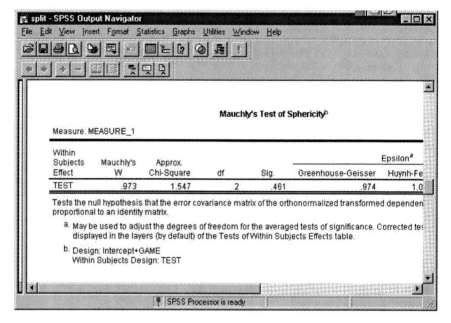

Figure 6.6: Mauchly's Test of Sphericity

Since we can assume sphericity, we will use the 7th table, which reports the "Tests of the Within-Subjects Effects" (See Figure 6.7). If our data had resulted in sphericity being broken, we would then interpret the results reported in the "Multivariate Tests" table listed earlier in the viewer file. We would examine the "Sig." For the Wilks' Lambda for the interaction and main effects for the treatment effects listed in "Multivariate tests" table listed earlier in the output file.

The "Tests of Within-Subjects Contrasts" list contrasts for the interaction (TEST*GAME) and the main effect of TEST across the levels of the between-participants levels (in this example there are two levels of the between-participant factor). The dependent variable is treated as a linear combination (adding up the repeated measures scores).

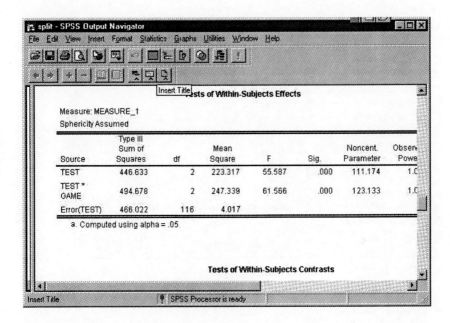

Figure 6.7: ANOVA Source Table for Tests Involving the Within-Subject Effects

The next table (the 9th table) lists the results of "Levene's Tests of the Equality of Error Variances, " also known as the test of homogeneity (See Figure 6.8). In this example there are three measurements of the dependent variable, so Levene's test

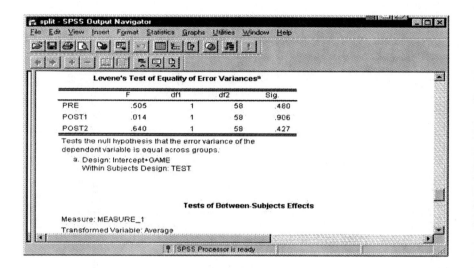

Figure 6.8: Levene's Test of Homogeneity in the SPSS® Output File

is conducted three separate times (for PRE, POST1, and POST2 scores). In our example, all of these tests are nonsignificant (.48, .906, and .427 > .01), so we have not broken the assumption of homogeneity of variances for the between-participants main effect (GAME). The next table lists the ANOVA results for the "Tests of Between-Subjects Effects" listing the appropriate error term and the main effect for our between-participants factor of GAME (See Figure 6.8). The "Estimated Marginal Means" are listed at the end of the print-out in two separate tables.

Since our interaction (TEST*GAME) was significant in this example (as listed in the "Tests of Within-Subjects Effects" table as F (2, 116) = 61.57, $MS_E = 4.02$, $p < .001$) we would conduct post hoc multiple comparisons across the 6 treatment conditions. When calculating the multiple comparisons we would use the means listed in the "Descriptives" table and the MS_{ERROR} and df_{ERROR} listed in the repeated measures table.

Split-plot ANOVA: Further Practice

For additional practice conduct the split-plot ANOVA on the following data. Notice that this design is a 2 x 2 split-plot design. Make sure to notice differences in the print-out between a 2 x 2 split-plot design compared with the 2 (between-participants) x 3 (repeated measures) split-plot ANOVA. There will be some tables that are not calculated when there are fewer than 3 levels of the repeated measures factor included in the design.

This research question examines the effects of taking a statistics course on the insanity of students. We have a 2 (statistics course vs. history course) x 2 (pretest-posttest) split-plot design. We will measure sanity on a 0-10 scale with 0 representing being sane and 10 representing total insanity. The statistics course is coded 1 and the history course is coded as 2. What do you conclude about the effects of a statistics course on insanity using this split-plot design and measuring insanity before and after course completion? Write up the results in an APA style results section.

SUBNUM	CLASS	PRETEST	POSTTEST
1.00	1.00	4.00	2.00
2.00	1.00	6.00	3.00
3.00	1.00	4.00	4.00
4.00	1.00	5.00	7.00
5.00	1.00	4.00	4.00
6.00	1.00	6.00	5.00
7.00	1.00	5.00	5.00
8.00	1.00	7.00	4.00
9.00	1.00	5.00	6.00
10.00	1.00	6.00	5.00
11.00	1.00	4.00	2.00

12.00	1.00	5.00	4.00
13.00	1.00	4.00	4.00
14.00	1.00	7.00	6.00
15.00	1.00	5.00	3.00
16.00	1.00	5.00	3.00
17.00	1.00	3.00	5.00
18.00	1.00	6.00	4.00
19.00	1.00	5.00	4.00
20.00	1.00	2.00	7.00
21.00	1.00	6.00	2.00
22.00	1.00	4.00	6.00
23.00	1.00	5.00	5.00
24.00	1.00	7.00	5.00
25.00	1.00	4.00	7.00
26.00	1.00	5.00	4.00
27.00	1.00	5.00	6.00
28.00	1.00	4.00	5.00
29.00	1.00	6.00	4.00
30.00	1.00	2.00	5.00
31.00	2.00	9.00	2.00
32.00	2.00	8.00	3.00
33.00	2.00	7.00	6.00
34.00	2.00	8.00	5.00
35.00	2.00	7.00	3.00
36.00	2.00	8.00	6.00
37.00	2.00	8.00	4.00
38.00	2.00	9.00	3.00
39.00	2.00	9.00	2.00
40.00	2.00	6.00	5.00
41.00	2.00	8.00	6.00
42.00	2.00	10.00	5.00
43.00	2.00	9.00	6.00

44.00	2.00	8.00	4.00
45.00	2.00	8.00	3.00
46.00	2.00	8.00	5.00
47.00	2.00	9.00	3.00
48.00	2.00	9.00	5.00
49.00	2.00	8.00	6.00
50.00	2.00	9.00	2.00
51.00	2.00	7.00	5.00
52.00	2.00	10.00	3.00
53.00	2.00	9.00	5.00
54.00	2.00	10.00	5.00
55.00	2.00	6.00	6.00
56.00	2.00	9.00	3.00
57.00	2.00	9.00	3.00
58.00	2.00	8.00	4.00
59.00	2.00	8.00	3.00
60.00	2.00	7.00	5.00

Chapter 7: Bivariate Correlation and Linear Regression

Bivariate Correlation

The command to conduct Pearson's Product Moment Correlation Coefficient (among two variables) is relatively straightforward, so this chapter will take a slightly different format. We will consider the research question, data, analysis, and interpreting the results as one section of the chapter. The more complex linear regression will be demonstrated and discussed using separate sections for each part of the research problem.

Our correlational design involves examining the relationship between number of cigarettes smoked on average per day (SMOKE) and a measure of physical well-being that involves a rating system based on participants' lung capacity, heart rate, and blood pressure. Our dependent variable (HEALTH) utilizes a 0 (Great Health) to 10 (Poor Health) scale. Our predictor variable (SMOKE) will range between 0 and 20.

PARTICIPANT	HEALTH	SMOKE
1.00	6.00	15.00
2.00	6.00	10.00
3.00	6.00	16.00
4.00	3.00	.00
5.00	2.00	.00
6.00	3.00	.00
7.00	5.00	8.00

8.00	4.00	7.00
9.00	3.00	.00
10.00	3.00	.00
11.00	5.00	1.00
12.00	6.00	7.00
13.00	4.00	5.00
14.00	4.00	2.00
15.00	5.00	9.00
16.00	4.00	2.00
17.00	6.00	6.00
18.00	3.00	1.00
19.00	5.00	10.00
20.00	5.00	11.00
21.00	3.00	4.00
22.00	6.00	15.00
23.00	5.00	6.00
24.00	5.00	9.00
25.00	6.00	8.00
26.00	5.00	8.00
27.00	6.00	13.00
28.00	5.00	2.00
29.00	3.00	.00
30.00	2.00	.00
31.00	2.00	.00
32.00	2.00	.00
33.00	6.00	16.00
34.00	4.00	4.00
35.00	7.00	13.00
36.00	2.00	.00
37.00	4.00	.00
38.00	5.00	11.00
39.00	4.00	8.00

40.00	2.00	.00
41.00	5.00	2.00
42.00	3.00	.00
43.00	2.00	.00
44.00	3.00	.00
45.00	4.00	.00
46.00	3.00	2.00
47.00	6.00	10.00
48.00	4.00	2.00
49.00	2.00	.00
50.00	3.00	.00
51.00	3.00	.00
52.00	3.00	.00
53.00	3.00	.00
54.00	3.00	.00
55.00	5.00	2.00
56.00	6.00	9.00
57.00	7.00	20.00
58.00	5.00	1.00
59.00	4.00	8.00
60.00	3.00	3.00

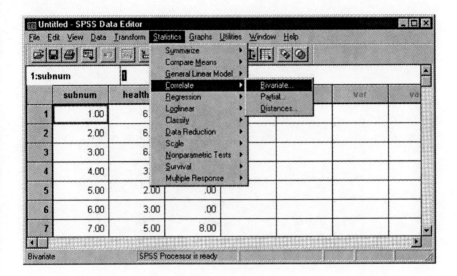

Figure 7.1: Selecting the Bivariate Correlation Procedure

To analyze this design we select the "Bivariate" analysis from the "Correlate" pull-down menu (See Figure 7.1). Double click the predictor variable name (SMOKE) and the dependent variable name (HEALTH) in the "Bivariate Correlation" window. The two variable names should appear in the "Variables" windowpane (See Figure 7.2). Next, click on the "Options" button, then click the "Means and standard deviations" check box, and then the "Continue" button. Finally, click the "OK" button and the results file will be calculated.

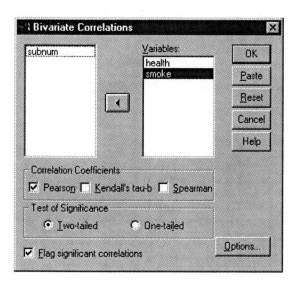

Figure 7.2: Selecting Variables

The output file has two tables. The first table reports the means and standard deviations for predictor variable (SMOKE) and the dependent variable (HEALTH). The second table is redundant, in that it lists each correlation coefficient (r) twice (See Figure 7.3). We will just consider the upper right-hand half of the "Correlations" table. This table reports the Pearson Correlation coefficient ($r = .83$), the 2-tailed significance level of this correlation coefficient ("Sig. (2-tailed)" < .001), and the number of valid observations used to calculate this coefficient (N=60). We evaluate the statistical significance of the correlation coefficient as we have all other statistics, comparing the reported significance level to our decision rule of a=.01. Since, the calculated probability of the correlation coefficient was less than our decision rule, we conclude that the relationship between SMOKE and HEALTH is statistical significant.

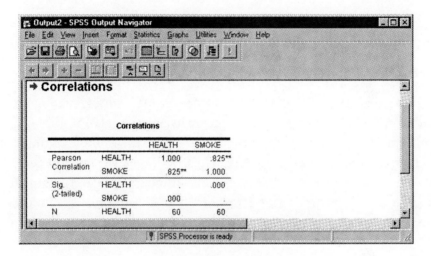

Figure 7.3: Correlation Table

Remember that the correlation coefficient tells us two things about the relationship between the predictor variable and dependent variable. The sign a *significant* coefficient tells us if the relationship is positive or negative. A positive relationship represents high values on the predictor variable *tend* to be associated with high values on the dependent variable and, likewise, low values on the predictor variable *tend* to be associated with low values on the dependent variable. A negative relationship represents that high values on the predictor variable *tend* to be associated with low values on the dependent variable and low values on the predictor variable *tend* to be associated with high values on the dependent variable. The value of a significant correlation coefficient represents the strength of the relationship between the two variables. The value of a correlation coefficient is 0.00 to 1.00, where 0.00 represents no relationship between the variables and 1.00 represents a perfect relationship. While it is possible to empirically derive a correlation coefficient of 0.00, the only way that we could have an empirically derived correlation of 1.00 is to correlate a variable with itself (which would be a useless correlation). We report the correlation coefficient as follows: r (58) $= .83, p < .001$.

Linear Regression: The Research Question and Data

Let's expand our research question to examine multiple predictors of our HEALTH measure. In addition to analyzing the relationship of cigarette smoking to HEALTH, we will also utilize the average number of hours spent exercising per week (range: 0-15), age in years, and gender. We are interested in determining if the number of cigarettes smoked predicts a person's rating of HEALTH after accounting for the other predictor variables. We collect the following data from a group of 60 people.

In order to answer this research question we will use a *hierarchical* regression model. In a hierarchical regression analysis, we specifically identify when each predictor is entered into the regression analysis. Since age and gender are participant characteristics we will enter both of these predictors in the *first block* of the analysis. Then we will enter the measure of exercise, and then finally the number of cigarettes smoked. With this analysis we will have three *blocks*. Be aware that there are also Forward, Backward, and Stepwise approaches to linear regression but the hierarchical method is usually the best approach.

SUBNUM	HEALTH	SMOKE	EXERCISE	AGE	GENDER
1.00	4.00	25.00	2.00	27.00	.00
2.00	3.00	31.00	.00	23.00	.00
3.00	4.00	27.00	1.00	31.00	.00
4.00	3.00	5.00	1.00	26.00	1.00
5.00	3.00	35.00	1.00	23.00	1.00
6.00	4.00	.00	.00	35.00	.00
7.00	7.00	13.00	7.00	44.00	1.00
8.00	4.00	18.00	2.00	35.00	.00

9.00	7.00	15.00	6.00	43.00	.00
10.00	3.00	13.00	.00	29.00	1.00
11.00	4.00	9.00	.00	29.00	1.00
12.00	6.00	17.00	2.00	41.00	1.00
13.00	4.00	18.00	.00	32.00	1.00
14.00	4.00	12.00	3.00	29.00	.00
15.00	5.00	37.00	2.00	33.00	1.00
16.00	6.00	27.00	3.00	43.00	1.00
17.00	3.00	3.00	.00	26.00	1.00
18.00	2.00	21.00	.00	19.00	1.00
19.00	6.00	1.00	4.00	40.00	.00
20.00	4.00	11.00	.00	33.00	1.00
21.00	4.00	30.00	.00	33.00	.00
22.00	5.00	8.00	2.00	33.00	.00
23.00	2.00	9.00	.00	19.00	.00
24.00	4.00	10.00	3.00	28.00	.00
25.00	4.00	15.00	1.00	32.00	.00
26.00	6.00	5.00	4.00	39.00	1.00
27.00	2.00	17.00	.00	23.00	1.00
28.00	4.00	38.00	.00	29.00	1.00
29.00	5.00	23.00	1.00	33.00	1.00
30.00	5.00	36.00	4.00	39.00	.00
31.00	2.00	5.00	.00	22.00	1.00
32.00	4.00	.00	.00	26.00	1.00
33.00	4.00	11.00	2.00	32.00	1.00
34.00	2.00	17.00	.00	18.00	.00
35.00	2.00	39.00	.00	26.00	.00
36.00	3.00	16.00	1.00	28.00	.00
37.00	6.00	15.00	6.00	37.00	.00
38.00	3.00	21.00	1.00	28.00	1.00
39.00	2.00	33.00	.00	20.00	1.00
40.00	3.00	30.00	.00	23.00	.00

41.00	3.00	32.00	1.00	29.00	1.00
42.00	6.00	37.00	3.00	45.00	.00
43.00	5.00	30.00	4.00	39.00	1.00
44.00	4.00	38.00	.00	27.00	.00
45.00	3.00	32.00	.00	23.00	1.00
46.00	3.00	20.00	.00	31.00	.00
47.00	6.00	17.00	6.00	38.00	1.00
48.00	4.00	35.00	.00	32.00	1.00
49.00	6.00	17.00	5.00	38.00	1.00
50.00	5.00	29.00	4.00	39.00	1.00
51.00	4.00	34.00	.00	34.00	.00
52.00	6.00	24.00	6.00	38.00	.00
53.00	2.00	11.00	.00	18.00	.00
54.00	4.00	10.00	3.00	31.00	.00
55.00	3.00	10.00	.00	26.00	.00
56.00	6.00	27.00	2.00	38.00	1.00
57.00	2.00	22.00	.00	25.00	.00
58.00	6.00	3.00	6.00	45.00	1.00
59.00	5.00	3.00	2.00	34.00	.00
60.00	5.00	28.00	3.00	33.00	.00

Linear Regression: The Command

Syntax Command

Following is the easiest syntax language for the linear regression example that we are using in this chapter.

```
REGRESSION
/DESCRIPTIVES MEAN STDDEV CORR SIG N
/MISSING LISTWISE
/STATISTICS COEFF OUTS R ANOVA CHANGE
/CRITERIA=PIN(.05) POUT(.10)
```

/NOORIGIN
/DEPENDENT health
/METHOD=ENTER age gender   /METHOD=ENTER exerci
/METHOD=ENTER smoke .

Menu Command

Calculating the linear regression equation using the SPSS® pull-down menus, we click on the "Statistics" option, the "Regression" option, and then the "Linear" option (See Figure 7.4). This will open the "Linear Regression" window, in which we will create the prediction model we are interested in testing (See Figure 7.5).

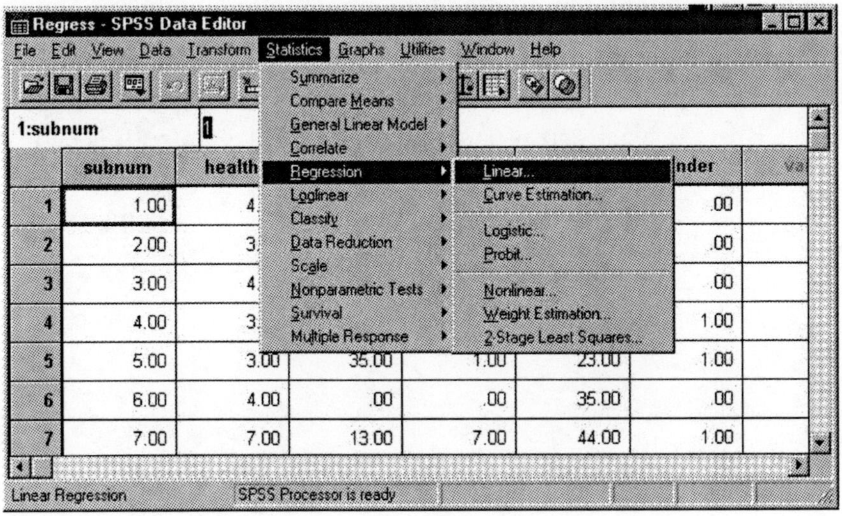

Figure 7.4: Selecting the Linear Regression Procedure

The Linear Regression window requires that we identify the dependent variable. In our example this is the HEALTH scaled score, so we highlight the "health" variable name in the variable list in the left-hand pane and click on the black arrow button located next to the "Dependent" windowpane. Next we need to request the order that the predictor variables will be entered into the equation. Since we are interested if the average number of cigarettes smoked predicts cardiovascular health, controlling for the other factors (e.g., age, gender, etc.), we will use the "Enter" method. As stated above, we will enter age and gender in the first hierarchical block, so highlight each of these variable names (one at a time) and click the black arrow button located next to the "Independent(s)" windowpane. Once both AGE and GENDER appear in this pane, click on the "Next" button located just above the "Independent(s)" pane, next to the informational message "Block 1 of 1." Now highlight the EXER variable name and click on the black arrow button next to the "Independent(s)" windowpane. Again, click on the "Next" button to move to the third and final block of the regression analysis. Once the informational message "Block 3 of 3" appears in the "Independent(s)" section of the window, highlight the SMOKE variable and click on the black arrow to send it to the "Independent(s)" pane.

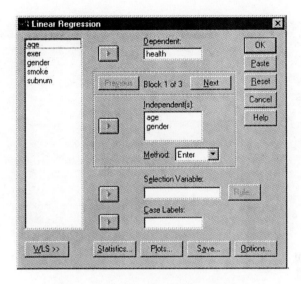

Figure 7.5: Linear Regression Window

Now we need to open the "Statistics" window by clicking the "Statistics" button at the bottom of the "Linear Regression" window. In addition to what is already requested, click on the "R Square Change" and "Descriptives" check boxes and then the "Continue" button to return to the "Linear Regression" window (See Figure 7.6). We are ready to run the regression analysis, so click the "OK" button and the analysis will be conducted.

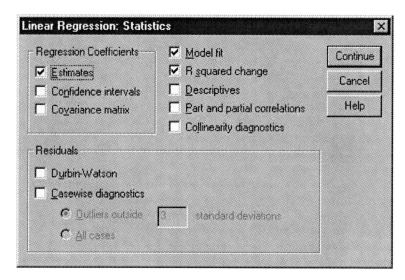

Figure 7.6: Linear Regression Statistics

Linear Regression: Interpreting the Results

The results of the analysis are reported in seven (7) tables. The first table reports the "Descriptive Statistics" we requested for all of the variables included in the analysis. This table is helpful when we report the results of the study, since it is required by all peer-reviewed journals that authors report means and standard deviations for all of the study variables. The second table listed is the "Correlations" table and lists the bivariate correlations (as discussed above) among all of the study variables. Again, this is useful for reporting the results of the study and to check for a statistical artifact called *multicolinearity*, which means that predictor variables are highly (significantly) correlated. For statistical reasons we want to avoid multicolinearity because one of the predictors may come out of the analysis as significant and another will be shown as nonsignificant, even if that may not be the case.

The third table simply lists the variables entered into the equation. It a good idea to take a look at this table to make sure that all of the predictor variables you want in the equation are actually entered in the equation. The next table is the "Model Summary," which lists the significance (in ANOVA terms) of the overall model steps (See Figure 7.7). At the first model (Model 1) the *F* statistic and the significance level listed is for the combination of both predictors entered at that step (i.e., both AGE and GENDER). This table is helpful because it evaluates the "change" in the equation as new predictors are entered into the equation. The significance of the change *F* tells us if the variance explained at that step is significant above and beyond that already explained by previously entered predictor variables. So, for our example, the third model shows that the predictor variable of SMOKE had a change significance level of *p* < .054 meaning that once we take into account the age, gender, and amount of exercise reported by our participants, the number of cigarettes smoked *does not* predict a persons health index (HEALTH) score.

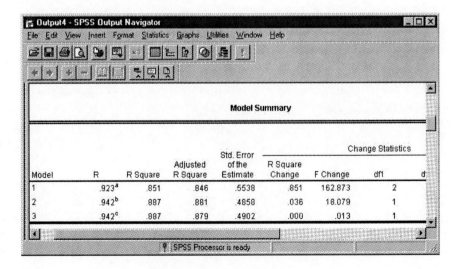

Figure 7.7: Regression Model Summary

The fifth table lists the ANOVA results for all of the predictor variables entered in the regression equation at that step. Unlike the "Change" table, this includes all of the predictor at each model, not just the new ones. So, the ANOVA results listed for the third model (Model 3) includes as treatment variance ("Regression" on the printout), variance from age, gender, amount of exercise, and number of cigarettes smoked.

The sixth table is the most important in the regression printout (See Figure 7.8). This table lists the "Coefficients" for each of the predictor variables individually. We need to reproduce this table when we report the results of our regression analysis. At a minimum, we must report the *Beta*, *t*, and *p* listed for each of the predictor variables. The *Beta* or regression weight and significance reported for each predictor variable in this table tells us if the predictor variable is significantly related to the dependent variable and how strong that relationship is, if in fact it is statistically significant. We often write the regression equation out as a prediction equation. **For our example we have no significant predictors so we would not write out the prediction equation.** But, if all predictors were significant we would write the equation as follows:

HEALTH = -.02 (AGE) + -.07(GENDER) + -.07(EXERCISE) + -.03(SMOKE)—6.049

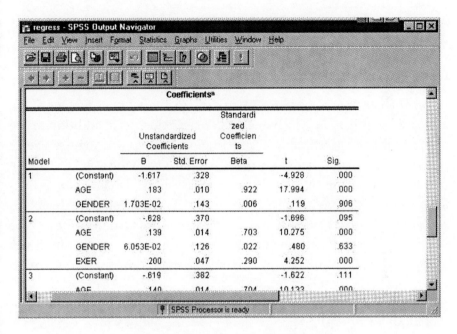

Figure 7.8: Regression Coefficients Table

Notice that the weights that are used in the prediction equation are the *B* or unstandardized regression weights, not the *Beta* weights. To predict a person's HEALTH score, we need only plug in the person's age, gender (0 or 1), the amount of exercise, and the number of cigarettes smoked, multiplying each by their respective regression weights. Again, this example has no significant predictors, so it would be inappropriate to use this equation – it is only for illustration.

The final table lists the variables not included in the regression equation at each step (or model) of the linear regression analysis. It is interesting to note that the SMOKE variable would have been significant (*p* < .041) had this variable been entered in the equation at the second step. But since we entered the SMOKE variable after all of the other variables (i.e., age, gender, and exercise), it was nonsignificant.

Linear Regression: Further Practice

For further practice you are attempting to predict scores on a driving test based on the following data from 60 participants. In addition to the road driving test (DRIVING SCORE), you measure the drivers' age in years (AGE), the number of years the have been driving (YEARS), and a written test over the rules of the road (TEST). The driving score ranges from 0=poor driving to 20= great driving; age ranges from 16 to 75; years range from 0 to 25 years; and written test scores range from 0% to 100%. Analyze the following data using the linear regression procedure and write up the results in an APA style Results section. Make sure to report the best prediction model.

SUBNUM	DRIVING SCORE	AGE	YEARS	TEST
1.00	10.00	53.00	4.00	18.00
2.00	10.00	53.00	15.00	12.00
3.00	11.00	55.00	14.00	32.00
4.00	9.00	51.00	5.00	8.00
5.00	7.00	21.00	3.00	.00
6.00	6.00	43.00	13.00	.00
7.00	9.00	61.00	19.00	20.00
8.00	9.00	64.00	24.00	3.00
9.00	8.00	26.00	22.00	9.00
10.00	10.00	32.00	6.00	25.00
11.00	9.00	40.00	16.00	9.00
12.00	8.00	68.00	3.00	9.00
13.00	6.00	31.00	6.00	.00
14.00	13.00	45.00	1.00	32.00
15.00	8.00	54.00	24.00	6.00

16.00	9.00	57.00	12.00	5.00
17.00	6.00	39.00	10.00	.00
18.00	10.00	45.00	20.00	30.00
19.00	8.00	57.00	5.00	.00
20.00	10.00	59.00	17.00	6.00
21.00	6.00	22.00	14.00	.00
22.00	9.00	32.00	16.00	14.00
23.00	6.00	64.00	6.00	.00
24.00	8.00	29.00	24.00	18.00
25.00	10.00	38.00	12.00	15.00
26.00	10.00	44.00	15.00	19.00
27.00	11.00	42.00	9.00	34.00
28.00	10.00	68.00	21.00	12.00
29.00	8.00	70.00	18.00	.00
30.00	10.00	45.00	15.00	26.00
31.00	8.00	54.00	4.00	9.00
32.00	13.00	55.00	7.00	45.00
33.00	13.00	56.00	23.00	31.00
34.00	9.00	19.00	14.00	3.00
35.00	10.00	55.00	4.00	4.00
36.00	7.00	67.00	.00	.00
37.00	8.00	54.00	.00	.00
38.00	7.00	61.00	23.00	.00
39.00	10.00	67.00	7.00	17.00
40.00	12.00	39.00	2.00	39.00
41.00	10.00	64.00	9.00	23.00
42.00	7.00	28.00	9.00	9.00
43.00	10.00	69.00	23.00	8.00
44.00	11.00	41.00	16.00	35.00
45.00	6.00	45.00	12.00	8.00
46.00	10.00	20.00	17.00	3.00
47.00	11.00	18.00	22.00	33.00

48.00	10.00	29.00	6.00	7.00
49.00	13.00	61.00	15.00	27.00
50.00	10.00	49.00	2.00	2.00
51.00	8.00	65.00	22.00	6.00
52.00	8.00	24.00	18.00	9.00
53.00	8.00	34.00	20.00	.00
54.00	11.00	31.00	15.00	35.00
55.00	10.00	18.00	5.00	27.00
56.00	12.00	18.00	10.00	31.00
57.00	9.00	40.00	3.00	2.00
58.00	6.00	67.00	19.00	.00
59.00	12.00	57.00	13.00	12.00
60.00	10.00	63.00	7.00	9.00

ABOUT THE AUTHOR

Dr. Zagumny is a Professor of Psychology at Tennessee Technological University in Cookeville, TN where he teaches undergraduate and graduate statistics and research methods courses. He has an active international research agenda in the area of psychosocial factors related to the prevention of HIV/AIDS. He is the American Director of the Collaborative Social Research Center with the Lower Silesian College of Education and University of Wroclaw in Poland. He is the author of over 30 professional articles and 50 professional presentations, workshops, and invited addresses. Prior to his appointment at Tennessee Tech, Dr. Zagumny served as the Director of Research and Evaluation at Community Mental Health of Michigan and as Research Specialist at the Medical College of Wisconsin. Dr. Zagumny received his M.A. and Ph.D. in psychology from Central Michigan University in Mt. Pleasant, MI and his B.S. in psychology from Aquinas College in Grand Rapids, MI.

Index

LaVergne, TN USA
24 August 2010
194478LV00001B/136/A

9 780595 189137